knits
for TEENS

knits
for TEENS

16
CONTEMPORARY DESIGNS
IN CASCADE YARNS
for Junior Sizes 3 to 15

lee gant

STACKPOLE BOOKS

Guilford, Connecticut

Published by Stackpole Books
An imprint of The Rowman & Littlefield Publishing Group, Inc.
4501 Forbes Blvd., Ste. 200
Lanham, MD 20706
www.stackpolebooks.com

Distributed by NATIONAL BOOK NETWORK
800-462-6420

British Library Cataloguing in Publication Information available

Library of Congress Cataloging-in-Publication Data
Names: Gant, Lee, author, compiler. | Cascade Yarns.
Title: Knits for teens : 16 contemporary designs in Cascade Yarns for junior sizes 3 to 15 / Lee Gant.
Description: First edition. | Guilford, Connecticut : Stackpole Books, 2019.
Identifiers: LCCN 2018035925 (print) | LCCN 2018037504 (ebook) | ISBN 9780811766180 (Electronic) | ISBN 9780811737104 (pbk. : alk. paper)
Subjects: LCSH: Knitting—Patterns. | Teenagers—Clothing.
Classification: LCC TT825 (ebook) | LCC TT825 .G264 2019 (print) | DDC 746.43/2041—dc23
LC record available at https://lccn.loc.gov/2018035925

First Edition

Printed in the United States of America

Contents

Acknowledgments

Once again, I would like to thank my photographer, Jonathan Kirker, for his patience, perseverance, and photography perfection.

To my models, Hailie, Anyssa, Francesca, Sami, and Karissa, I thank you for your modeling expertise and exceptional beauty. You make this book what it is.

And a special thank you to Cascade Yarns for allowing me to see my vision come to life.

Introduction

I love yarn.

I love the way it feels slipping through my fingers, the way it feels against my skin. I like the bounce of the fabric when I knit a sweater or a coat or socks or a scarf. I've been known to place a skein under my nose and inhale. It makes me happy.

I especially love Cascade Yarns. Their 220 Superwash works up beautifully in lots of different gauges. I used a size 7 needle for the cabled sweaters and the zip-up hoodie, and a size 3 with the same yarn for the cardigan coat. And talk about colors! With at least 150 to choose from, you might go bonkers trying to decide. If you're not a wool lover, Cascade Yarns carries cotton, acrylic, linen, silk, llama, alpaca, and all the beautiful blends they create. I love the look and feel of small-needle knits, so if I had to choose, Heritage 150 would be probably my favorite. The easy-care merino/nylon blend is soft and squishy and a dream to wear against your skin.

As a follow-up to *Knits for Girls and Young Juniors*, I hope you enjoy these fashion-forward designs that girls in their teens and twenties will want to wear. *Knits for Teens* gives them something to be excited about and, hopefully, a reason to want to learn to knit. I chose Cascade because I love everything about all of their yarns . . . and they're wonderful people to work with.

Should you have any questions, feel free to contact me at leegant101@yahoo.com.

With Love in Every Stitch,
Lee

Joining hands with

GALLERY

Cabled Red Dress

page 24

Cardigan Coat
page 32

Circle Skirt

page 40

Cropped Top

page 44

Francesca's Cabled
Sweater

page 54

Jade Top
page 61

Open-Back Sweater

page 66

Pretty in Pink

page 71

Sarasota V-Neck
Shirt

page 74

Simple Shift
with Two Belts

page 80

Reversible
Cabled
Brioche Belt

page 86

Twisted Rib
Tie Belt

page 88

Summer Dress

page 90

Sunset and Lace

page 96

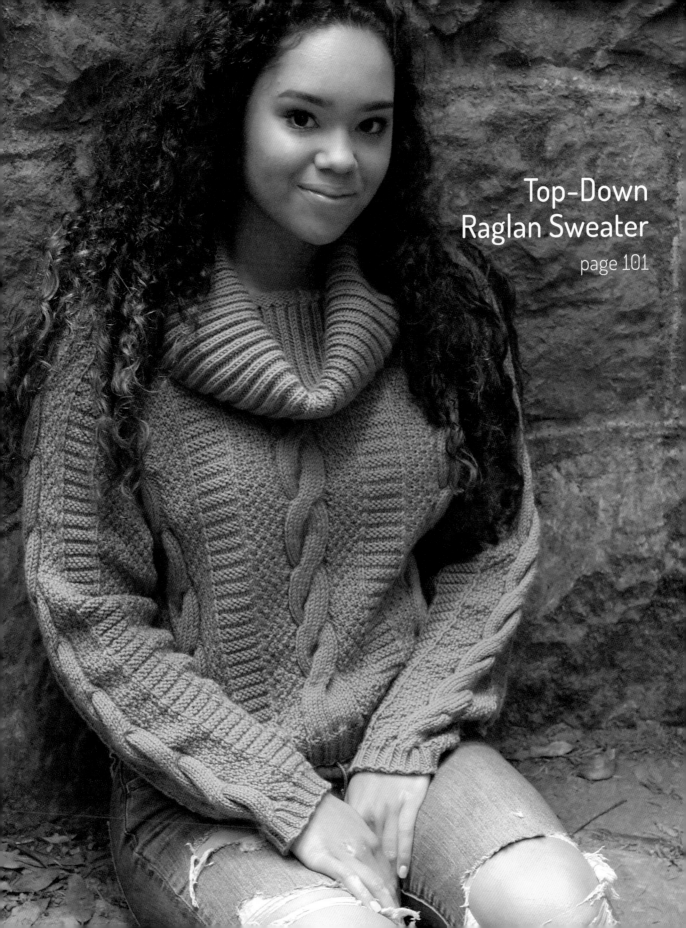

Top-Down
Raglan Sweater

page 101

Woven Stitch
Summer Top

page 106

Zip-Up Hoodie
page 110

PATTERNS

Cabled Red Dress

Beautifully shaped and cabled, this stunning dress is a must-have for any teen's wardrobe.

SIZES

Junior 3 (5, 7, 9) (11, 13, 15)

Instructions are written for size 3; all other sizes are in parentheses.

FINISHED MEASUREMENTS

Chest: 32 (35, 37, 38) (38½, 39, 41) in / 81.5 (89, 94, 96.5) (98, 99, 104) cm

Waist: 27 (27½, 28, 30) (31½, 33, 36) in / 68.5 (70, 71, 76) (80, 84, 91.5) cm

Hips: 31 (35, 36, 38) (39½, 41, 42) in / 78.5 (89, 91.5, 96.5) (100.5, 104, 106.5) cm

Back to waist length: 13½ (14½, 15, 15½) (15½, 16, 16) in / 34.5 (37, 38, 39.5) (39.5, 40.5, 40.5) cm

Total length: 30½ (32½, 33, 34) (34½, 35, 35½) in / 77.5 (82.5, 84, 86.5) (87.5, 89, 90) cm

YARN

Cascade Yarns Anchor Bay; 3.5 oz / 100 g each approx. 262 yd / 240 m; 50% cotton, 50% superwash merino wool

- 7 (7, 7, 8) (8, 9, 9) skeins #06 Scarlet

MATERIALS

- Size US 6 / 4 mm 24 in / 60 cm circular needle (*or size to obtain gauge*)
- Size US 4 / 3.5 mm 24 in / 60 cm circular needle
- Size US 4 / 3.5 mm 16 in / 40 cm circular needle (for neckband)
- Tapestry needle
- Waste yarn
- Pin-type stitch markers
- Ring-type stitch marker

GAUGE

24 sts and 30 rows to 4 in / 10 cm in St st

STITCH GUIDE

C6B. Slip next 3 sts onto CN and hold at back, k3, then k3 from CN.

C6F. Slip next 3 sts onto CN and hold at front, k3, then k3 from CN.

T4B. Slip next st onto CN and hold at back, k3, then p1 st from CN.

T4F. Slip next 3 sts onto CN and hold at front, p1, then k3 from CN.

T5B. Slip next 2 sts onto CN and hold at back, k3, then p2 from CN.

T5F. Slip next 3 sts onto CN and hold at front, p2, then k3 from CN.

Three-needle bind-off. Turn pieces inside out and place live stitches on 2 parallel needles. Then knit 2 stitches together, one from each of the parallel needles. Knit another 2 stitches together, one from each needle. You now have 2 stitches on your right needle; use your left needle to pull the first stitch over the second and off the needle (one stitch bound off). Continue binding off in this manner (k2tog, bind off 1).

STITCH PATTERNS

Right Side Cable (to right of center) (over 29 sts)
Row 1 (RS): P2, k3, p4, T5F, [k1, p1] 3 times, k1, C6F, p2.
Row 2 (WS): K2, p6, [k1, p1] 3 times, k1, p3, k6, p3, k2.
Row 3: P2, k3, p6, k3, [k1, p1] 3 times, k1, k6, p2.
Row 4: K2, p6, [k1, p1] 3 times, k1, p3, k6, p3, k2.
Row 5: P2, k3, p6, k3, [k1, p1] 3 times, k1, k6, p2.
Row 6: K2, p6, [k1, p1] 3 times, k1, p3, k6, p3, k2.
Row 7: P2, k3, p4, T5B, [k1, p1] 3 times, k1, C6F, p2.
Row 8: K2, p6, [k1, p1] 4 times, k1, p3, k4, p3, k2.
Row 9: P2, k3, p2, T5B, [k1, p1] 3 times, k1, T5B, k3, p2.
Row 10: K2, p3, k2, p3, [k1, p1] 4 times, k1, p3, k2, p3, k2.
Row 11: P2, k3, T5B, [k1, p1] 3 times, k1, T5B, p2, k3, p2.
Row 12: K2, p3, k4, p3, [k1, p1] 4 times, k1, p6, k2.
Row 13: P2, C6B, [k1, p1] 3 times, k1, T5B, p4, k3, p2.
Row 14: K2, p3, k6, p3, [k1, p1] 3 times, k1, p6, k2.
Row 15: P2, k6, [k1, p1] 3 times, k1, k3, p6, k3, p2.
Row 16: K2, p3, k6, p3, [k1, p1] 3 times, k1, p6, k2.
Row 17: P2, k6, [k1, p1] 3 times, k1, k3, p6, k3, p2.
Row 18: K2, p3, k6, p3, [k1, p1] 3 times, k1, p6, k2.
Row 19: P2, C6B, [k1, p1] 3 times, k1, T5F, p4, k3, p2.
Row 20: K2, p3, k4, p3, [k1, p1] 4 times, k1, p6, k2.
Row 21: P2, k3, T5F, [k1, p1] 3 times, k1, T5F, p2, k3, p2.
Row 22: K2, p3, k2, p3, [k1, p1] 4 times, k1, p3, k2, p3, k2.
Row 23: P2, k3, p2, T5F, [k1, p1] 3 times, k1, T5F, k3, p2.
Row 24: K2, p6, [k1, p1] 4 times, k1, p3, k4, p3, k2.
Repeat rows 1–24 for pattern.

Center Panel (over 38 sts)
Row 1 (RS): K4, p6, C6B, p2, k2, p2, C6F, p6, k4.
Row 2 and all WS rows: Knit the knits and purl the purls.
Row 3: K4, p5, T4B, T4F, p1, k2, p1, T4B, T4F, p5, k4.
Row 5: K4, p4, T4B, p2, T4F, k2, T4B, p2, T4F, p4, k4.
Row 7: K1, T4F, p2, T4B, p4, k8, p4, T4F, p2, T4B, k1.
Row 9: K1, p1, T4F, T4B, p5, k8, p5, T4F, T4B, p1, k1.
Row 11: K1, p2, C6F, p6, k8, p6, C6B, p2, k1.
Row 13: K1, p2, k6, p6, k8, p6, k6, p2, k1.
Row 15: Same as row 13.
Row 17: K1, p2, C6F, p6, k8, p6, C6B, p2, k1.
Row 19: K1, p1, T4B, T4F, p5, k8, p5, T4B, T4F, p1, k1.
Row 21: K1, T4B, p2, T4F, p4, k8, p4, T4B, p2, T4F, k1.
Row 23: K4, p4, T4F, p2, T4B, k2, T4F, p2, T4B, p4, k4.
Row 25: K4, p5, T4F, T4B, p1, k2, p1, T4F, T4B, p5, k4.
Row 27: K4, p6, C6B, p2, k2, p2, C6F, p6, k4.
Row 29: K4, p6, k6, p2, k2, p2, k6, p6, k4.
Row 31: Same as row 29.
Row 32: Knit the knits and purl the purls.
Repeat rows 1–32 for pattern.

Left Side Cable (to left of center) (over 29 sts)
Row 1 (RS): P2, C6B, [k1, p1] 3 times, k1, T5B, p4, k3, p2.
Row 2 (WS): K2, p3, k6, p3, [k1, p1] 3 times, k1, p6, k2.
Row 3: P2, k6, [k1, p1] 3 times, k1, k3, p6, k3, p2.
Row 4: K2, p3, k6, p3, [k1, p1] 3 times, k1, p6, k2.
Row 5: P2, k6, [k1, p1] 3 times, k1, k3, p6, k3, p2.
Row 6: K2, p3, k6, p3, [k1, p1] 3 times, k1, p6, k2.
Row 7: P2, C6B, [k1, p1] 3 times, k1, T5F, p4, k3, p2.
Row 8: K2, p3, k4, p3, [k1, p1] 4 times, k1, p6, k2.
Row 9: P2, k3, T5F, [k1, p1] 3 times, k1, T5F, p2, k3, p2.
Row 10: K2, p3, k2, p3, [k1, p1] 4 times, k1, p3, k2, p3, k2.
Row 11: P2, k3, p2, T5F, [k1, p1] 3 times, k1, T5F, k3, p2.
Row 12: K2, p6, [k1, p1] 4 times, k1, p3, k4, p3, k2.
Row 13: P2, k3, p4, T5F, [k1, p1] 3 times, k1, C6F, p2.
Row 14: K2, p6, [k1, p1] 3 times, k1, p3, k6, p3, k2.
Row 15: P2, k3, p6, k3, [k1, p1] 3 times, k1, k6, p2.
Row 16: K2, p6, [k1, p1] 3 times, k1, p3, k6, p3, k2.
Row 17: P2, k3, p6, k3, [k1, p1] 3 times, k1, k6, p2.
Row 18: K2, p6, [k1, p1] 3 times, k1, p3, k6, p3, k2.
Row 19: P2, k3, p4, T5B, [k1, p1] 3 times, k1, C6F, p2.
Row 20: K2, p6, [k1, p1] 4 times, k1, p3, k4, p3, k2.

Row 21: P2, k3, p2, T5B, [k1, p1] 3 times, k1, T5B, k3, p2.
Row 22: K2, p3, k2, p3, [k1, p1] 4 times, k1, p3, k2, p3, k2.
Row 23: P2, k3, T5B, [k1, p1] 3 times, k1, T5B, p2, k3, p2.
Row 24: K2, p3, k4, p3, [k1, p1] 4 times, k1, p6, k2.
Repeat rows 1–24 for pattern.

PATTERN NOTES

- Pattern is worked flat from the bottom up.
- Sleeves are picked up and worked flat to cuff.
- Neckband is picked up and worked in the round.

DRESS FRONT

With smaller needle, cast on 115 (127, 130, 136) (142, 145, 148) sts.

Row 1 (WS): [P1, k2] repeat to last stitch, p1.
Row 2 (RS): [K1, p2] repeat to last st, k1.

Repeat rows 1 and 2 until rib measures 2½ in / 6.5 cm (or desired length). On last WS row, decrease 1 (1, 2, 2) (2, 1, 0) sts to 114 (126, 128, 134) (140, 144, 148) sts.

Change to larger needles and begin pattern as follows:

Row 1 (RS): K2, p7 (13, 14, 17) (20, 22, 24), place marker, p2, k3, p4, T5F, [k1, p1] 3 times, k1, C6F, p2, place marker, k4, p6, C6B, p2, k2, p2, C6F, p6, k4, place marker, p2, C6B, [k1, p1] 3 times, k1, T5B, p4, k3, p2, place marker, p7 (13, 14, 17) (20, 22, 24), k2.

Row 2 (WS): P2, k7 (13, 14, 17) (20, 22, 24), slip marker, k2, p3, k6, p3, [k1, p1] 3 times, k1, p6, k2, slip marker, work row 2 of Center Panel, slip marker, k2, p6, [k1, p1] 3 times, k1, k6, p3, k2, slip marker, k7 (13, 14, 17) (20, 22, 24), p2.

Row 3 (RS): K2, p7 (13, 14, 17) (20, 22, 24), work row 3 of Right Side Cable, work row 3 of Center Panel, work row 3 of Left Side Cable, p7 (13, 14, 17) (20, 22, 24), k2.

Row 4 (WS): P2, k7 (13, 14, 17) (20, 22, 24), work row 3 of Left Side Cable, work row 3 of Center Panel, work row 3 of Right Side Cable, k7 (13, 14, 17) (20, 22, 24), p2.

Work pattern as established until piece from beginning measures 9½ (9½, 9, 9) (9, 9, 10) in / 24 (24, 23, 23) (23, 23, 25.5) cm. End having completed a WS row. Begin counting rows for decreases now.

Hip to Waist Shaping

To work a WS decrease row: P2, ssk, work to within last 4 sts of end of row, k2tog, p2.

Work decrease row every 6th WS row 7 (10, 9, 10) (11, 11, 11) times total to 100 (106, 110, 114) (118, 122, 126) sts. Work with no further decreases until piece from beginning measures 16½ (17, 17½, 17½) (18, 18½, 19) in / 42 (43, 44.5, 44.5) (45.5, 47, 48.5) cm (or desired length to waist). Hang a pin-type marker somewhere across the row for ease in measuring.

Waist to Bust Shaping

To work a WS increase row: P2, M1, work to last 2 sts, M1, p2.

To work a RS increase row: K2, M1P work to last 2 sts, M1P, k2.

Work an increase row every 6th (6th, 6th, 6th) (7th, 7th, 6th) row 9 (10, 10, 10) (9, 9, 10) times total to 118 (126, 130, 134) (136, 140, 146) sts. Work with no further increases until piece from waist measures 7 (8, 8, 8½) (8½, 8½, 8½) in / 18 (20.5, 20.5, 21.5) (21.5, 21.5, 21.5) cm (or desired length to underarm). End having completed a RS row.

Armhole Shaping

Next row (WS): Bind off 6 (7, 7, 8) (8, 8, 8) sts, work across row (hang a pin-type marker somewhere in the middle of the row for ease in measuring).

Next row (RS): Bind off 6 (7, 7, 8) (8, 8, 8) sts, work across.

Next row (WS): K1, ssk, work patterns as established across to last 3 sts, k2tog, k1.

Next row (RS): Work across as established.

Repeat last 2 rows 5 (5, 6, 6) (6, 7, 7) times more to 94 (100, 102, 104) (106, 108, 114) sts.**

Note: Size 3 will need to adjust side pattern instructions to accommodate the loss of one stitch.

Work even until armholes measure (measure from the hanging pin) 3 (3, 3½, 3½) (3½, 4, 4) in / 7.5 (7.5, 9, 9) (9, 10, 10) cm. End having completed a WS row.

Front Neck Shaping

Next row (RS): Work across 28 (31, 32, 32) (34, 35, 38) sts, bind off center cable pattern over next 38 sts, work across remaining 28 (31, 32, 32) (34, 35, 38) sts. Place left shoulder sts on a holder or waste yarn.

Working on right shoulder only, work as follows:

Next row (WS): Work to last 3 sts, p2togtbl (through back loop), p1.

Next row (RS): K2, work across row.

Repeat last 2 rows 5 (6, 7, 7) (8, 9, 11) times more to 22 (24, 24, 24) (25, 25, 26) sts. Work even if necessary until length of armhole measures 6½ (6½, 7, 7) (7,

7½, 7½) in / 16.5 (16.5, 18, 18) (18, 19, 19) cm. Place sts on a holder or waste yarn.

Join new yarn on WS at neck edge and work as follows:
WS: P1, p2tog, work across row.
Next row (RS): Work to last 2 sts, k2.
Repeat last 2 rows 5 (6, 7, 7) (8, 9, 11) times more to 22 (24, 24, 24) (25, 25, 26) sts. Work even if necessary until length of armhole measures 6½ (6½, 7, 7) (7, 7½, 7½) in / 16.5 (16.5, 18, 18) (18, 19, 19) cm. Place on a holder or waste yarn.

DRESS BACK
Work same as for Front to **. [96 (102, 104, 108) (112, 114, 122) sts]
Work even until armholes measures (measure from the hanging pin) 4 (4, 4½, 4½) (4½, 4½, 4½) in / 10 (10, 11.5, 11.5) (11.5, 11.5, 11.5) cm. End having completed a WS row.

Back Neck Shaping
Next row (RS): Work across 28 (31, 32, 32) (34, 35, 38) sts, bind off center cable pattern over next 38 sts, work across remaining 28 (31, 32, 32) (34, 35, 38) sts. Place left shoulder sts on a holder or waste yarn.

Working on right shoulder only, work as follows:
WS: Work to last 3 sts, p2togtbl (through back loop), p1.
Next row (RS): K2, work across row.
Repeat last 2 rows 5 (6, 7, 7) (8, 9, 11) times more to 22 (24, 24, 24) (25, 25, 26) sts. Work even (if necessary) until length of armhole measures 6½ (6½, 7, 7) (7, 7½, 7½) in / 16.5 (16.5, 18, 18) (18, 19, 19) cm. Place sts on a holder or waste yarn.

Join new yarn on WS at neck edge and work as follows:
WS: P1, p2tog, work across row.
Next row (RS): Work to last 2 sts, k2.
Repeat last 2 rows 5 (6, 7, 7) (8, 9, 11) times more to 22 (24, 24, 24) (25, 25, 26) sts. Work even (if necessary) until length of armhole measures 6½ (6½, 7, 7) (7, 7½, 7½) in / 16.5 (16.5, 18, 18) (18, 19, 19) cm.

Use the three-needle bind-off to connect the shoulders together.

SLEEVES
Note: Sleeves will be worked in short rows as you incorporate the bound-off sts, then worked across all sts. This forms a little extra fabric at the top of the sleeve. The original number of picked-up sts will remain the same. It is important to center the 60 sts at top of sleeve for cable pattern.

At underarm, from the RS, *not* including the 12 (14, 14, 16) (16, 16, 16) bound-off sts, pick up and knit 15 (15, 18, 18) (18, 21, 21) sts, place marker, pick up and knit 30 sts to shoulder, pick up and knit 30 sts, place marker, pick up and knit 15 (15, 18, 18) (18, 21, 21) sts to beginning of bind-off: 90 (90, 96, 96) (96, 102, 102) sts. Turn.

Begin Sleeve Cable pattern:
Note: Cable pattern is worked over center 60 sts on background of reverse stockinette stitch, with 2

selvedge sts at each end after all bound-off sts are incorporated.

The 60 cable stitches are marked in brackets in the instructions below. Once pattern is established, follow the instructions in the Sleeve Cable pattern sidebar for the bracketed stitches to continue working the sleeve.

Set-up row (WS): K15 (15, 18, 18) (18, 21, 21) slip marker, [k2, p6, k10, p6, k2, p8, k2, p6, k10, p6, k2], slip marker, work to within one stitch of end of row. With tip of left needle, pick up first bound-off stitch, slip the last stitch from right needle to left, and work the 2 sts together; turn.

Row 1 (RS): P15 (15, 18, 18) (18, 21, 21), [p2, C6F, p10, C6F, p2, k8, p2 C6F, p10, C6F, p2], p14 (14, 17, 17) (17, 20, 20), pick up bound-off stitch with left needle and purl it together with last stitch; turn.

Row 2 and all WS rows: Knit the knits and purl the purls, picking up last stitch with bound-off st and knitting them together as before; turn.

Row 3: P15 (15, 18, 18) (18, 21, 21), [p2, k6, p10, k6, p2, k8, p2, k6, p10, k6, p2], p14 (14, 17, 17) (17, 20, 20),

pick up bound-off stitch with left needle and purl it together with last stitch; turn.

Row 5: P15 (15, 18, 18) (18, 21, 21), [p2, k6, p10, k6, p2, k8, p2, k6, p10, k6, p2], p14 (14, 17, 17) (17, 20, 20), pick up bound-off stitch with left needle and purl it together with last stitch; turn.

Note: Size 3 will have no more bound-off sts; all other sizes will turn and work one or two more pick-up rows.

Once sleeve has incorporated all bound-off sts, k2 at beginning and end of every RS row, p2 at beginning and end of every WS row.

Work row 6 as established.

Row 7: P15 (15, 18, 18) (18, 21, 21), [p2, C6F, p10, C6F, p2, k8, p2, C6F, p10, C6F, p2], p14 (14, 17, 17) (17, 20, 20). Turn.

Continue working rows as established (directions for Sleeve Cable pattern in sidebar) until all sts are used up from the bind-off, keeping cable pattern correct, and begin counting your rows for decreases now.

To work a RS decrease row: K2, p2tog, work to last 4 sts, p2tog, k2.

To work a WS decrease row: P2, ssk, work to last 4 sts, k2tog, p2.

Work a decrease row every 7th (7th, 6th, 6th) (7th, 6th, 6th) row 13 (13, 16, 16) (16, 19, 19) times to 64 sts. Keep a k2 at beginning and end of every RS row (purl on WS) and work with no further decreases (if necessary) until sleeve (from shoulder) measures 14½ (15, 15½, 16) (16½, 17, 17) in / 37 (38, 39.5, 40.5) (42, 43, 43) cm (or desired length to cuff). End having completed a RS row.

SLEEVE CABLE PATTERN
(60 sts of cable pattern only)

Set-up row (WS): K2, p6, k10, p6, k2, p8, k2, p6, k10, p6, k2

Row 1 (RS): P2, C6F, p10, C6F, p2, k8, p2 C6F, p10, C6F, p2

Row 2 and all WS rows: knit the knits and purl the purls

Row 3: P2, k6, p10, k6, p2, k8, p2, k6, p10, k6, p2

Row 5: P2, k6, p10, k6, p2, k8, p2, k6, p10, k6, p2

Row 7: P2, C6F, p10, C6F, p2, k8, p2, C6F, p10, C6F, p2

Row 9: P1, T4B, T4F, p8, T4B, T4F, p1, k8, p1, T4B, T4F, p8, T4B, T4F, p1

Row 11: T4B, p2, T4F, p6, T4B, p2, T4F, k8, T4B, p2, T4F, p6, T4B, p2,T4F

Row 13: K3, p4, T4F, p4, T4B, p4, k14, p4, T4F, p4, T4B, p4, k3

Row 15: K3, p5, T4F, p2, T4B, p5, k14, p5, T4F, p2, T4B, p5, k3

Row 17: K3, p6, T4F, T4B, p6, k14, p6, T4F, T4B, p6, k3

Row 19: K3, p7, C6B, p7, k14, p7, C6B, p7, k3

Row 21: K3, p6, T4B, T4F, p6, k14, p6, T4B, T4F, p6, k3

Row 23: K3, p5, T4B, p2, T4F, p5, k14, p5, T4B, p2, T4F, p5, k3

Row 25: K3, p4, T4B, p4, T4F, p4, k14, p4, T4B, p4, T4F, p4, k3

Row 27: T4F, p2, T4B, p6, T4F, p2, T4B, k8, T4F, p2, T4B, p6, T4F, p2, T4B

Row 29: P1, T4F, T4B, p8, T4F, T4B, p1, k8, p1, T4F, T4B, p8, T4F, T4B, p1

Row 30: Knit the knits and purl the purls.

Repeat rows 1–30 for cable pattern.

Change to smaller needle

Row 1 (WS): [P1, k2] repeat to last stitch, p1.

Row 2 (RS): [K1, p2] repeat to last st, k1.

Repeat rows 1 and 2 for pattern.

When cuff measures 2 (2, 2½, 3) (3, 3, 3) in / 5 (5, 6.5, 7) (7, 7, 7) cm (or desired length), bind off in rib.

Make other sleeve to match.

Sew side and underarm seams from the right side using a mattress stitch.

NECKBAND

With US 4 / 3.5 mm 16 in / 40 cm circular needle, begin at back of left shoulder and pick up and knit 3 out of 4 sts. Make sure your number is a multiple of 3; adjust if necessary on next round.

Place a marker and work rib pattern as follows: [k1, p2] repeat around.

Repeat last round until neckband measures 1–1½ in / 2.5–4 cm or desired length. Bind off in rib.

FINISHING

Weave in any ends and steam lightly, or block according to directions on ball band.

Cardigan Coat

Wrap yourself in this long diamonds-and-cables sweater coat. No side shaping, simple cables, and beautiful stitch definition give this piece its exquisite look.

SIZES

Small (Medium, Large)
Junior 3–5 (7–9, 11–15)
Limited by the large pattern repeat, needle size determines finished measurements.
Directions are written for size Small; all other sizes are in parentheses.

FINISHED MEASUREMENTS

Chest: 36 (40, 44) in / 91.5 (101.5, 112) cm
Length: 45 in / 114 cm

YARN

Cascade 220 Superwash; 3.5 oz / 100 g each approx. 220 yd / 200 m; 100% superwash wool
- 11 (12, 12) skeins #856 Aporto

MATERIALS

- For size Small: Size US 3 / 3.25 mm (*or size to obtain gauge*) needles as follows: 29 in / 73 cm or longer circular needle, 16 in / 40 cm circular needle for sleeves, and a set of double-pointed needles for working cuffs in the round. To pick up the front border, you will need several long needles (borrow from friends).
- For size Medium: Size US 5 / 3.75 mm needles (*or size to obtain gauge*), in lengths same as above for Small size.
- For size Large: Size US 7 / 4.5 mm needles (*or size to obtain gauge*), in lengths same as above for Small size.
- Cable needle
- Tapestry needle
- Waste yarn
- Several pin-type markers
- 1 ring-type marker

GAUGE

For size Small: 24 sts and 30 rows to 4 in / 10 cm in St st

For size Medium: 22 sts and 28 rows to 4 in / 10 cm in St st

For size Large: 20 sts and 26 rows to 4 in / 10 cm in St st

STITCH GUIDE

Cr4R. Slip next 2 sts onto CN and hold at back, k2, then p2 from CN.

Cr4L. Slip next 2 sts onto CN and hold at front, p2, then k2 from CN.

C4B. Slip next 2 sts onto CN and hold at back, k2, then k2 from CN.

C4F. Slip next 2 sts onto CN and hold at front, k2, then k2 from CN.

Three-needle bind-off. Turn pieces inside out and place live stitches on 2 parallel needles. Then knit 2 stitches together, one from each of the parallel needles. Knit another 2 stitches together, one from each needle. You now have 2 stitches on your right needle; use your left needle to pull the first stitch over the second and off the needle (one stitch bound off). Continue binding off in this manner (k2tog, bind off 1).

STITCH PATTERNS

Reverse St st in the Round
Purl every round.

1x1 Twisted Rib
Row 1: [K1b, p1b] repeat to end of row.
Row 2: Knit the knits and purl the purls, working all sts through the back loop.

PATTERN NOTES

- It's helpful to know that the diamonds move over 2 sts every RS row, and the little cables twist every 4th row. Once you get going, you shouldn't need the row directions, except where the cables intersect with the diamonds.
- The twisted rib and coat are both worked with the same needle size. The difference in gauge has been accounted for in the numbers so the rib won't pull in.
- The cables will pull the coat to a smaller gauge than your swatch in St st.

- Back and Front are worked in one piece to armholes, then worked separately.
- Three-needle bind-off is used at shoulders.
- Sleeves are picked up and knit in the round from the shoulders down.
- Front border is picked up and worked in twisted rib using several size 3 needles, as the length of the pick-up is approx. 90 in / 228 cm.
- Twisted rib hem and front borders are the only places with twisted sts; all other sts are worked in the usual way.

BACK AND FRONT

Cast on 345 sts.

Note: Since the pattern looks the same on both sides, mark the RS for ease in picking up front band later and setting up the pattern.

Set-up row (WS): [P1, k1] to last st, p1.

Next row (RS): K1, p1b, [k1b, p1b] to last st, k1.

Next row: P1, [k1b, p1b] to last 2 sts, k1b, p1.

Keeping first and last st of every row untwisted, repeat last 2 rows for 3 in / 7.5 cm of twisted rib (or desired length). End having completed a WS row (all twisted sts end here).

Decrease row (RS): K1, k2tog, [k3, k2tog, k2, k2tog] to end of row. [268 sts]

Begin Diamond and Cable pattern (multiple of 52+8):

Next row (pattern set-up row, WS): P1, k1, p6, [k44, p8] 4 times, k44, p6, k1, p1.

Row 1 (RS): K1, p1, k4, [Cr4L, p40, Cr4R, k4] 5 times, p1, k1.

Row 2 and all WS rows: Knit the knits and purl the purls.

Row 3: K1, p1, [C4B, p2, Cr4L, p36, Cr4R, p2] 5 times, C4F, p1, k1.

Row 5: K1, p1, [k4, p4, Cr4L, p32, Cr4R, p4] 5 times, k4, p1, k1.

Row 7: K1, p1, [C4B, p6, Cr4L, p28, Cr4R, p6] 5 times, C4F, p1, k1.

Row 9: K1, p1, [k4, p8, Cr4L, p24, Cr4R, p8] 5 times, k4, p1, k1.

Row 11: K1, p1, [C4B, p10, Cr4L, p20, Cr4R, p10] 5 times, C4F, p1, k1.

Row 13: K1, p1, [k4, p12, Cr4L, p16, Cr4R, p12] 5 times, k4, p1, k1.

Row 15: K1, p1, [C4B, p14, Cr4L, p12, Cr4R, p14] 5 times, C4F, p1, k1.

Row 17: K1, p1, [k4, p16, Cr4L, p8, Cr4R, p16] 5 times, k4, p1, k1.

Row 19: K1, p1, [C4B, p18, Cr4L, p4, Cr4R, p18] 5 times, C4F, p1, k1.

Row 21: K1, p1, [k4, p20, Cr4L, Cr4R, p20] 5 times, k4, p1, k1.

Row 23: K1, p1, [C4B, p22] 10 times, C4F, p1, k1.

Row 25: K1, p1, [k4, p20, C4B, C4F, p20] 5 times, k4, p1, k1.

Row 27: K1, p1, [C4B, p18, Cr4R, k4, Cr4L, p18] 5 times, C4F, p1, k1.

Row 29: K1, p1, [k4, p16, Cr4R, p2, C4B, p2, Cr4L, p16] 5 times, k4, p1, k1.

Row 31: K1, p1, [k4, p14, Cr4R, p4, k4, p4, Cr4L, p14] 5 times, C4F, p1, k1.

Row 33: K1, p1, [k4, p12, Cr4R, p6, C4B, p6. Cr4L, p12] 5 times, k4, p1, k1.

Row 35: K1, p1, [C4B, p10, Cr4R, p8, k4, p8, Cr4L, p10] 5 times, C4F, p1, k1.

Row 37: K1, p1, [k4, p8, Cr4R, p10, C4B, p10. Cr4L, p8] 5 times, k4, p1, k1.

Row 39: K1, p1, [C4B, p6, Cr4R, p12, k4, p12, Cr4L, p6] 5 times, C4F, p1, k1.

Row 41: K1, p1, [k4, p4, Cr4R, p14, C4B, p14. Cr4L, p4] 5 times, k4, p1, k1.

Row 43: K1, p1, [C4B, p2, Cr4R, p16, k4, p16, Cr4L, p2] 5 times, C4F, p1, k1.

Row 45: K1, p1, [k4, Cr4R, p18, C4B, p18. Cr4L] 5 times, k4, p1, k1.

Row 47: K1, p1, C4B, k2, [p20, k4, p20, Cr4L, Cr4R] 4 times, p20, k4, p20, k2, C4F, p1, k1.

Row 49: K1, p1, k6, p20 [C4B, p22] 8 times, C4B, p20, k6, p1, k1.

Row 51: K1, p1, C4B, k2, p20, [k4, p20, C4B, C4F, p20] 4 times, k4, p20, k2, C4F, p1, k1.

Row 53: K1, p1, [k4, Cr4L, p18, C4B, p18, Cr4R] 5 times, k4, p1, k1.

Row 55: K1, p1, [C4B, p2, Cr4L, p16, k4, p16, Cr4R, p2] 5 times, C4F, p1, k1.

Row 57: K1, p1, [k4, p4, Cr4L, p14, C4B, p14, Cr4R, p4] 5 times, k4, p1, k1.

Row 59: K1, p1, [C4B, p6, Cr4L, p12, k4, p12, Cr4R, p6] 5 times, C4F, p1, k1.

Row 61: K1, p1, [k4, p8, Cr4L, p10, C4B, p10, Cr4R, p8] 5 times, k4, p1, k1.

Row 63: K1, p1, [C4B, p10, Cr4L, p8, k4, p8, Cr4R, p10] 5 times, C4F, p1, k1.

Row 65: K1, p1, [k4, p12, Cr4L, p6, C4B, p6, Cr4R, p12] 5 times, k4, p1, k1.

Row 67: K1, p1, [C4B, p14, Cr4L, p4, k4, p4, Cr4R, p14] 5 times, C4F, p1, k1.

Row 69: K1, p1, [k4, p16, Cr4L, p2, C4B, p2, Cr4R, p16] 5 times, k4, p1, k1.

Row 71: K1, p1, [C4B, p18, Cr4L, k4, Cr4R, p18] 5 times, C4F, p1, k1.

Row 72: Knit the knits and purl the purls.

Work rows 21–72 for pattern until piece from beginning measures 38 in / 96.5 cm (or desired length to underarm). End having completed a WS row. *Make note of this row.*

Next row (RS): Divide for front and back. *Hang a pin-type marker somewhere across both fronts and the back for ease in measuring.*

Work in pattern across 61 sts for right front, bind off 12 sts, work across 122 sts for back, bind off 12 sts, work across last 61 sts for left front.

Notes:

- Both fronts (and back) will have a k3 on RS and a p3 on WS *at side edges* for decorative detail and ease in picking up sleeves.
- Depending on where your pattern ends, a "work 2tog" could be knit or purl. Use whichever works into the pattern best.

Left Front

Next row (WS): Keeping pattern correct, work across row to last 3 sts, p3.

Next row (RS): K3, work 2tog, work pattern to last 8 sts, work 2tog, work last 6 sts as established.

Repeat last 2 rows 5 times more until 49 sts remain. Armhole decreases complete.

Work one WS row.

Continue decreases for sloped front edge as follows:

Next row (RS): Work pattern across to last 8 sts, work 2tog, work last 6 sts as established.

Next row (WS): Knit the knits and purl the purls.

Repeat last 2 rows until 29 sts remain. Continue with no further decreases (if necessary) until armhole measures 7 in / 18 cm from bind-off. Cut yarn and place sts on a holder or waste yarn.

Right Front

Begin on WS at underarm at sleeve edge, join new yarn and work as follows:

(WS): P3, keep rest of pattern correct and work across.

Next row (RS): Work first 6 sts as established, work 2tog, work across to last 5 sts, work 2tog, k3.

Repeat last 2 rows 5 times more until 49 sts remain. Armhole decreases complete.

Work one WS row.

Continue decreases for sloped front edge as follows:

Next row (RS): Work first 6 sts as established, work 2tog, work to last 3 sts, k3.

Next row (WS): Knit the knits and purl the purls.

Repeat last 2 rows until 29 sts remain. Continue with no further decreases (if necessary) until armhole

measures 7 in / 18 cm from bind-off. Cut yarn and place sts on a holder or waste yarn.

Back

Join new yarn at WS.

(WS): P3, pattern across to last 3 sts, p3.

Next row (RS): K3, work 2tog, work in pattern across to last 5 sts, work 2tog, k3.

Repeat last 2 rows 5 times more until 110 sts remain. Armhole decreases complete.

Continue with no further decreases until armhole measures 5½ in / 14 cm. End having completed a WS row.

Neck Shaping

Next row (RS): Work across 33 sts, bind off center 44 sts, continue in pattern on last 33 sts.

Left Shoulder

Next row (WS): Work across to last st, p1.
Next row (RS): K1, work 2tog, work in pattern to end.
Repeat last 2 rows 3 times more until 29 sts remain.
  Work even if necessary, until armhole measures same as front. Cut yarn and place sts on a holder or waste yarn.

Right Shoulder

Join new yarn on WS at neck edge.
(WS): P1, work across as established.
Next row (RS): Work pattern to last 3 sts, work 2tog, k1.
Repeat last 2 rows 3 times more until 29 sts remain.
  Work even if necessary, until armhole measures same as front.
Use the three-needle bind-off to connect the shoulder sts.

FRONT BAND

With long circular needles, begin at bottom right front and pick up and knit one st at edge of every row around entire front, back, and down other front. Don't bother counting sts. Just make sure to pick up every one. Work in twisted rib (all sts worked through the back loop) until band measures 1½–2 in / 4–5 cm (or desired width). Bind off *loosely* in [k1, p1] rib (not through the back loop).

SLEEVES

Note: As the sleeves are worked in reverse St st (purl every round), the gauge should now match your swatch.

With 16 in / 40 cm circular needle, begin at center of underarm and pick up and knit 6 sts from bind-off, then 50 (45, 43) sts to center shoulder, 50 (45, 43) sts to bind-off, and last 6 sts of bind-off. Place beg-of-rnd marker and continue as follows:

Rnd 1: P4, p2tog, k1, purl to last 7 sts, k1, p2tog, p4.

Next rnd: P3, p2tog, k1, purl to last 6 sts, k1, p2tog, p3.

Next rnd: P2, p2tog, k1, purl to last 5 sts, k1, p2tog, p2.

Next rnd: P1, p2tog, k1, purl to last 4 sts, k1, p2tog, p1.

Next rnd: P2tog, k1, purl to last 3 sts, k1, p2tog.

Next rnd: K2tog, purl to last 2 sts, ssk. Bound-off sts decreased away and 100 (90, 86) sts remain.

To work a decrease rnd: K1, p2tog, purl to last 3 sts, p2tog, k1.

Keeping one knit st at the beginning and end of every round and the rest in reverse St st (purl every round), work a decrease round every 5th (7th, 10th) round 12 (7, 5) times. Continue with decreases and begin Diamond and Cable pattern on 76 sts as follows:

Rnd 1: K1, p33, k8, p33, k1.

Rnd 2: K1, p 31, Cr4R, k4, Cr4L, p31, k1.

Rnd 3 and every odd-numbered rnd: Knit the knits and purl the purls.

Rnd 4: K1, p29, Cr4R, p2, C4B, p2, Cr4L, p29, k1.

Rnd 6: K1, p26, Cr4R, p4, k4, p4, Cr4L, p26, k1.

Rnd 8: K1, p24, Cr4R, p6, C4B, p6, Cr4L, p24, k1.

Rnd 10: K1, p2tog, p20, Cr4R, p8, k4, p8, Cr4L, p20, p2tog, k1.

Rnd 12: K1, p19, Cr4R, p10, C4B, p10, Cr4L, p19, k1.

Rnd 14: K1, p17, Cr4R, p12, k4, p12, Cr4L, p17, k1.

Rnd 16: K1, p14, Cr4R, p14, C4B, p14, Cr4L, p14, k1.

Rnd 18: K1, p12, Cr4R, p16, k4, p16, Cr4L, p12, k1.

Rnd 20: K1, p2tog, p8, Cr4R, p18, C4B, p18, Cr4L, p8, p2tog, k1.

Rnd 22: K1, p7, Cr4R, p20, k4, p20, Cr4L, p7, k1.

Rnd 24: K1, p7, Cr4L, p20, C4B, p20, Cr4R, p7, k1.

Rnd 26: K1, p8, Cr4L, p18, k4, p18, Cr4R, p8, k1.

Rnd 28: K1, p10, Cr4L, p16, C4B, p16, Cr4R, p10, k1.

Rnd 30: K1, p2tog, p10, Cr4L, p14, k4, p14, Cr4R, p10, p2tog, k1.

Rnd 32: K1, p13, Cr4L, p12, C4B, p12, Cr4R, p13, k1.

Rnd 34: K1, p15, Cr4L, p10, k4, p10, Cr4R, p15, k1.

Rnd 36: K1, p16, Cr4L, p8, C4B, p8, Cr4R, p16, k1.

Rnd 38: K1, p18, Cr4L, p6, k4, p6, Cr4R, p18, k1.

Rnd 40: K1, p2tog, p18, Cr4L, p4, C4B, p4, Cr4R, p18, p2tog, k1. *Decreases for size Small end here.* [60 sts remain.]

Rnd 42: K1, p21, Cr4L, p2, k4, p2, Cr4R, p21, k1.

Rnd 44: K1, p23, Cr4L, C4B, Cr4R, p23, k1.

Rnd 45: Knit the knits and purl the purls.

Diamond and Cable pattern complete. Begin cuff for size Small. For sizes Medium and Large, continue decreases in reverse St st until sleeve measures desired length less cuff or until (56, 52) sts remain; or if sleeve becomes long enough, decrease ahead of time evenly around to (56, 52) sts. Make a note, so that you can match on other sleeve.

Cuff

Work in twisted rib for 2–3 in / 5–7.5 cm (or desired length). Bind off loosely in regular rib (not through the back loop).

Make other sleeve to match.

FINISHING

Weave in any ends and steam lightly, or block according to directions on ball band.

Circle Skirt

This full-circle skater skirt is knit in the round with pattern detail at the waist, with or without elastic in the casing.

SIZES
Juniors 3 (5, 7, 9) (11, 13, 15)
Instructions are written for size 3; all other sizes are in parentheses.

FINISHED MEASUREMENTS
Waist: 24 (24½, 25, 27) (28½, 30, 32) in / 61 (62, 63.5, 68.5) (72.5, 76, 81.5) cm
Length from waist: 16½ (17, 17, 18) (18½, 18½, 18½) in / 42 (43, 43, 45.5) (47, 47, 47) cm

YARN
Heritage Silk #5672 Real Black Yarn; 3.5 oz / 100 g each approx. 437 yds / 400 meters; 85% superwash merino wool / 15% silk
  • 3 skeins (all sizes)

MATERIALS
  • Size US 3 / 3.25 mm 40 in / 101.5 cm circular needle (*or size to obtain gauge*)
  • Size US 3 / 3.25 mm 24 in / 60 cm circular needle
  • 3 in / 7.5 cm wide elastic (optional)
  • Tapestry needle
  • Waste yarn
  • Pin-type markers, ring-type markers
  • Size G or H / 4 or 5 mm crochet hook for provisional cast-on chain (no other crochet skills needed)

GAUGE
26 sts and 36 rows to 4 in / 10 cm in St st

STITCH GUIDE

Provisional Cast-on. With waste yarn and crochet hook, chain desired number of stitches plus a few more and finish off. Pick up and knit stitches through the back loop of the chain. For those who don't want to crochet, cast on desired number of stitches and knit a few rows in waste yarn before continuing in project yarn.

PATTERN NOTES

- As the skirt increases, the only counting you have to do is every 7th round. Then relax and enjoy 6 knit rounds.
- The skirt will automatically circle no matter what length you desire.

SKIRT

Begin at waist with 24 in / 60 cm needle and crochet hook and provisionally cast on 156 (160, 164, 176) (186, 196, 208) sts. Place a marker and join into a round, being careful not to twist sts.

Knit 6 rnds.

Note: For all sizes, every 7th round will increase by 32 sts.

Rnd 7: Work increase round as follows for your size:

Size 3: K7, [k4, M1], k7, [k4, M1] 30 times, k7, [k4, M1], k7. [188 sts]

Size 5: [K5, M1] 32 times. [192 sts]

Size 7: K2, [k5, M1] 32 times, k2. [196 sts]

Size 9: K4, [k5, M1], k4, [k5, M1] 30 times, k4, [k5, M1], k4. [208 sts]

Size 11: K6, [k5, M1], k7, [k5, M1] 30 times, k7, [k5, M1], k6. [218 sts]

Size 13: K2, [k6, M1] 32 times, k2. [228 sts]

Size 15: K4, [k6, M1], k4, [k6, M1] 30 times, k4, [k6, M1], k4. [240 sts]

Knit 6 rnds.

Increase next round as before, *except* add one stitch before each M1 as follows:

Size 3: K7, [k5, M1], k7, [k5, M1] 30 times, k7, [k5, M1], k7. [220 sts]

Size 5: [K6, M1] 32 times. [224 sts]

Size 7: K2, [k6, M1] 32 times, k2. [228 sts]

Size 9: K4, [k6, M1], k4, [k6, M1] 30 times, k4, [k6, M1], k4. [240 sts]

Size 11: K6, [k6, M1], k7, [k6, M1] 30 times, k7, [k6, M1], k6. [250 sts]

Size 13: K2, [k7, M1] 32 times, k2. [260 sts]

Size 15: K4, [k7, M1], k4, [k7, M1] 30 times, k4, [k6, M1], k4. [272 sts]

Knit 6 rnds.

Increase next round as before, *except* add one stitch before each M1 as follows:

Size 3: K7, [k6, M1], k7, [k6, M1] 30 times, k7, [k6, M1], k7. [252 sts]

Size 5: [K7, M1] 32 times. [256 sts]

Size 7: K2, [k7, M1] 32 times, k2. [260 sts]

Size 9: K4, [k7, M1], k4, [k7, M1] 30 times, k4, [k7, M1], k4. [272 sts]

Size 11: K6, [k7, M1], k7, [k7, M1] 30 times, k7, [k7, M1], k6. [282 sts]

Size 13: K2, [k8, M1] 32 times, k2. [292 sts]

Size 15: K4, [k8, M1], k4, [k8, M1] 30 times, k4, [k7, M1], k4. [304 sts]

Work an increase round as established (adding one stitch before each M1) every 7th round until skirt measures approx. 16½ (17, 17, 18) (18½, 18½, 18½) in / 42 (43, 43, 45.5) (47, 47, 47) cm from cast-on (or de-sired length from waist). Use 40 in / 101.5 cm needle when sts become too crowded.

Next rnd: Purl all sts.

Next 2 rnds: Knit all sts.

Repeat last 3 rnds once more, then purl 1 rnd and bind off loosely knitwise.

With 24 in / 60 cm needle, unpick provisional cast-on, join new yarn (keep beginning of round marker) and *purl 1 rnd, knit 2 rnds. Repeat from * once more, then purl 1 rnd decreasing one stitch (p2tog) at end of rnd. [155 (159, 163, 175) (185, 195, 207) sts remain.]

Begin Waistband pattern (on an odd number of sts) for all sizes as follows:

Rnd 1: K1, [yo, slip 1, k1, yo, psso (pass the slipped st over the k1 and the yo)] around.

Rnd 2: K1, drop yo from previous rnd, [k2 (if it's easier, go ahead and knit the second stitch through the back loop), drop yo] to last 2 sts, k2.

Rnd 3: K2, [yo, sl 1, k1, yo, psso] to last st, k1.

Rnd 4: [K2, drop yo] to last 3 sts, k3.

Work rnds 1–4 until band measures 4½ in / 11.5 cm.
   End after completing a round 2 or 4.
Next rnd: Purl all sts
Next 2 rnds: Knit all sts.
Repeat last 3 rnds once more, then purl 1 rnd.

Skirt Facing
Knit in rounds until facing measures 4½ in / 11.4 cm
   (or same width as waistband pattern). Bind off very
   loosely knitwise.

FINISHING

For optional elastic insertion, cut elastic approx. 1 in /
   2.5 cm shorter than waist measurement. Stitch elastic ends together and insert into folded-over casing.
   Whipstitch casing loosely to the skirt from the inside.
Weave in any loose ends and steam lightly, or block
   according to directions on ball band.

Cropped Top

This sleeveless top with a decorative bottom border and V-back can be cropped or worked longer if you choose.

SIZES

Juniors 3 (5, 7, 9) (11, 13, 15)
Instructions are written for size 3; all other sizes are in parentheses.

FINISHED MEASUREMENTS

Chest: 29 (32, 34, 35) (35½, 36, 38) in / 73.5 (81.5, 86.5, 89) (90, 91.5, 96.5) cm
Length: 15 (15½, 16, 17) (17½, 18, 18½) in / 38 (39.5, 40.5, 43) (44.5, 45.5, 47) cm
Cropped length: 13 (13½, 14, 15) (15½, 16, 16½) in / 33 (34.5, 35.5, 38) (39.5, 40.5, 42) cm

YARN

Heritage Silk #5672 Real Black Yarn; 3.5 oz / 100 g each approx. 437 yds / 400 meters; 85% superwash merino wool / 15% silk
*   2 skeins (all sizes)

MATERIALS

*   Size US 3 / 3.25 mm 24 in / 60 cm circular needle (*or size to obtain gauge*)
*   Size US 3 / 3.25 mm 16 in / 40 cm circular needle
*   Tapestry needle
*   Waste yarn
*   Ring-type markers.
*   2 pin-type markers

GAUGE

26 sts and 36 rows to 4 in / 10 cm in St st

STITCH GUIDE

Three-needle bind-off. Turn pieces inside out and place live stitches on 2 parallel needles. Then knit 2 stitches together, one from each of the parallel needles. Knit another 2 stitches together, one from each needle. You now have 2 stitches on your right needle; use your left needle to pull the first stitch over the second and off the needle (one stitch bound off). Continue binding off in this manner (k2tog, bind off 1).

PATTERN NOTES

- Worked in the round to armholes, front and back worked separately.
- Sleeve borders picked up and worked in the round.

BODY

Begin at center back of bottom edge and cast on 189 (207, 221, 227) (231, 235, 247) sts.

Place marker and join into a round, being careful not to twist sts.

Next rnd: Purl all sts.

Next 2 rnds: Knit all sts.

Repeat last 3 rnds once more, then purl 1 rnd.

Begin pattern (on an odd number of sts) for all sizes as follows:

Rnd 1: K1, [yo, sl 1, k1, yo, psso (pass the slipped st over the knit 1 and the yo)] around.

Rnd 2: K1, drop yo from previous rnd, [k2 (if it's easier, knit the second stitch through the back loop), drop yo] to last 2 sts, k2.

Rnd 3: K2, [yo, sl 1, k1, yo, psso] to last st, k1.

Rnd 4: [K2, drop yo] to last 3 sts, k3.

Work rnds 1–4 until band measures approximately 5 (5, 5, 5) (5, 5½, 6) in / 13 (13, 13, 13) (13, 14, 15) cm. End after completing a round 4.

Set-up pattern at center back:

Before beginning, hang a pin-type marker after the first 13 (13, 15, 15) (15, 15, 17) sts and another 12 (12, 14, 14) (14, 14, 16) sts from the end of round marker. (These sts will remain in pattern, and the pin-type markers will help you remember.)

Rnd 1: Work in pattern over first 13 (13, 15, 15) (15, 15, 17) sts, knit next 34 (39, 40, 42) (43, 44, 45) sts, place side marker, knit 96 (104, 112, 114) (116, 118, 124) for front, place side marker, knit 34 (39, 40, 42) (43, 44, 45) sts to hanging marker, sl 1, k1, yo, psso, [yo, sl 1, k1, yo, psso] 2 times. At end of rnd, before center marker, M1 (use a lifted increase).

Each pattern at center back should now have 13 (13, 15, 15) (15, 15, 17) sts.

Next rnd: Work rnd 2 of pattern over first 13 (13, 15, 15) (15, 15, 17) sts, knit around to last 13 (13, 15, 15) (15, 15, 17) sts, keeping pattern correct, work pattern over last 12 (12, 14, 14) (14, 14, 16) sts to last st, k1. *Always knit the last st of the round and the first st as well; this is where the back will split later.*

Continue working pattern as established across center back sts and stockinette st for all others until piece from beginning measures 6½ (7, 7, 8) (8, 8½, 9) in / 16.5 (18, 18, 20.5) (20.5, 21.5, 23) cm for cropped top, or add 2 in / 5 cm for a longer look (*or desired length to armhole*).

Divide for front and back:

On next rnd, knit to first side marker and place 94 (104, 110, 114) (116, 118, 124) back sts on waste yarn for later. *Keep center back marker in place.*

FRONT

Work as follows on front 96 (104, 112, 114) (116, 118, 124) sts only.

Armhole Shaping

(RS): Bind off 6 sts, then knit across row. *Hang a pin-type marker somewhere across this row for ease in measuring armhole.*

Next row (WS): Bind off 6 sts, purl across row.

Next row (RS): K1, ssk, knit to last 3 sts, k2tog, k1.

Next row: Purl.

Repeat last 2 rows 6 times more to 70 (78, 86, 88) (90, 92, 98) sts.

When work from armhole shaping measures 4½ (4½, 5, 5) (5½, 5½, 5½) in / 11.5 (11.5, 13, 13) (14, 14, 14,) cm, decrease 1 st by p2tog on last WS row to 69 (77, 85, 87) (89, 91, 97) sts.

Begin pattern as follows:

Row 1 (RS): K1, [yo, sl 1, k1, yo, psso (pass the slipped st over the knit 1 and the yo)] repeat around.

Row 2: [P2, drop yo] to last st, p1.

Row 3: K2, [yo, sl 1, k1, yo, psso] to last st, k1.

Row 4: P3, [drop yo, p2] repeat around.

Work rows 1–4 until band measures 2 in / 5 cm or total length of armhole is 6½ (6½, 7, 7) (7½, 7½, 7½). in /

16.5 (16.5, 18, 18) (19, 19, 19) cm. End having completed a WS row.

Next row: Knit across first 17 (19, 21, 21) (22, 22, 22) sts, bind off next 35 (39, 43, 45) (45, 47, 53) sts for center neck, then knit across rem 17 (19, 21, 21) (22, 22, 22) sts. Place shoulder sts on separate holders or waste yarn.

BACK

Note: Back will be divided into right and left sections, with armhole shaping and back decreases worked at same time. Keep markers separating pattern sts from St st.

Right Back

Place first 47 (52, 55, 57) (58, 59, 62) sts from holder (to center marker) onto needle. Join yarn on RS and bind off 6 sts, knit to last 15 (15, 17, 17) (17, 17, 19) sts, k2tog, slip marker, work pattern across last 13 (13, 15, 15) (15, 15, 17) sts.

Next row (WS): Work in pattern over first 13 (13, 15, 15) (15, 15, 17) sts, purl to end.

Next row (RS): K1, ssk, knit to last 15 (15, 17, 17) (17, 17, 19) sts, k2tog, work pattern across last 13 (13, 15, 15) (15, 15, 17) sts.

Repeat last 2 rows 6 times more. [13 total sts decreased at armhole edge] Armhole decreases are now complete.

Continue working a k2tog before pattern sts on every RS row until 17 (19, 21, 21) (22, 22, 22) sts remain. When armhole measures 6½ (6½, 7, 7) (7½, 7½, 7½) in / 16.5 (16.5, 18, 18) (19, 19, 19) cm, place sts on a holder or waste yarn.

Left Back

Join yarn on WS and bind off purlwise first 6 sts, purl across to last 13 (13, 15, 15) (15, 15, 17) sts, work pattern as established.

Next row (RS): Work pattern over first 13 (13, 15, 15) (15, 15, 17) sts, ssk, knit to last 3 sts, k2tog, k1.

Next row (WS): Purl across to last 13 (13, 15, 15) (15, 17) sts, work pattern as established.

Repeat last 2 rows 6 times more. [13 total sts decreased at armhole edge.] Armhole decreases now complete.

Continue working an ssk after pattern sts on every RS row until 17 (19, 21, 21) (22, 22, 22) sts remain. When armhole measures 6½ (6½, 7, 7) (7½, 7½, 7½) in / 16.5 (16.5, 18, 18) (19, 19, 19) cm, place sts on a holder or waste yarn.

Use the three-needle bind-off to connect 17 (19, 21, 21) (22, 22, 22) shoulder sts (from the wrong side) to front shoulder sts.

Armhole Edging

With 16 in / 40 cm circular needle, begin at underarm and pick up and knit 3 out of 4 sts around (except knit one stitch for every row at underarm decreases). Place a marker and purl one round, knit 2 rounds, purl one round, then bind off knitwise.

FINISHING

Weave in all ends and steam lightly, or block according to directions on ball band.

El Cielo Sweater

Soft-as-a-cloud, extra roomy, and oversized, this cropped top with hemmed bottom and ribbed turtleneck is sure to make your girl's "favorite" clothing rotation.

SIZES
One size for all Juniors

FINISHED MEASUREMENTS
Chest: 54 in / 137 cm
Length: 19 in / 48.5 cm

YARN
Cascade El Cielo; 3.5 oz / 100 g each approx. 579.6 yd / 530 meters; 89% superfine alpaca, 11% nylon
- 2 skeins #05 Ecru

MATERIALS
- Size US 6 / 4 mm 24–36 in / 61–91.5 cm circular needle (*or size to obtain gauge*)
- Size US 6 / 4 mm 16 in / 40 cm circular needle
- Size US 6 / 4 mm double-pointed needles (or any needles for knitting cuffs in the rnd)
- Tapestry needle
- Waste yarn
- Pin-type markers
- Ring-type markers, 2 colors
- Optional crochet hook size H / 5 mm (for cast-on chain only; no other crochet skills needed)

GAUGE
20 sts and 28 rows to 4 in / 10 cm in St st

STITCH GUIDE
Provisional cast-on. With waste yarn and crochet hook, chain desired number of stitches plus a few more and finish off. Pick up and knit stitches through the back loop of the chain. For those who don't want to crochet, cast on desired number of stitches and knit a few rows in waste yarn before continuing in project yarn.

Three-needle bind-off. Turn pieces inside out and place live stitches on 2 parallel needles. Then knit 2 stitches together, one from each of the parallel needles. Knit another 2 stitches together, one from each needle. You now have 2 stitches on your right needle; use your left needle to pull the first stitch over the second and off the needle (one stitch bound off). Continue binding off in this manner (k2tog, bind off 1).

Yf. Yarn forward; move the yarn in front of the working needle as if to purl.

W&t. Wrap and turn; slip the next stitch, bring the yarn to the front (or back if a purl row), then put the stitch back on the left needle, turn and work back across next row. Some stitches will be left unworked.

PATTERN NOTES

- Worked in the round to armholes; sleeves and neck picked up and knit in the round.
- The crochet chain provisional cast-on will make it easier to locate the cast-on sts when you turn up the bottom hem. Any cast-on will do, but then you'll have to stitch the hem later, as the sts of a long-tail cast-on will be nearly impossible to locate.

BODY

With crochet hook, chain 240 (or cast on 240 sts using any method, if you are prepared to sew the hem later).

With longer circular needle, knit a stitch into each chain, place a marker (this will be the center back) and join into a rnd, being careful not to twist sts.

Knit for 2 in / 5 cm.

Next rnd (turning rnd): [Yf, k2tog] repeat around.

Next rnd: Knit (including one st in each yf).

Next rnd: K60, place marker, k120, place other side marker, k60 to beg-of-rnd "center back" marker.

Knit for 2 in / 5 cm.

If you have a crochet cast-on, continue with directions to fold and join hem. Otherwise, jump ahead to in-crease-round directions.

To fold and join hem for crochet cast-on: With tip of right needle, *pick up chain from cast-on and place on left needle, then knit it together with next stitch;

repeat from * around. The hem is now folded and joined to the body with original 240 sts. Continue in St st and work increases as follows:

To work an increase round: *Knit to within 1 st of side marker, M1, k1, slip marker, M1, repeat from * once more at other side, and complete rnd. [4 sts increased per rnd at side edges]

Work an increase rnd every 7th rnd 8 times to 272 sts. (You don't have to count, and certainly don't rip back if you miss a decrease rnd; a few sts or rows off here and there won't make a bit of difference.) Piece from beg (with hem folded) should measure approx. 10 in / 25.5 cm (or 12 in / 30.5 cm from beg if hem has not been folded and attached). Continue with no further increases for 1 in / 2.5 cm (or desired length to armholes). End at center back marker.

Divide for front and back:
Knit past first side marker to other side marker. Place last 136 sts *just worked* to an extra needle (or waste yarn) for front.

BACK (now worked in St st rows)
Continue across back sts, removing beg-of-rnd marker as you come to it.

Beginning with a purl row, continue in St st until piece from armhole divide measures 6½ in / 16.5 cm. End having completed a WS row.

Next row (RS): Work across 91 sts. Place last 46 sts *just worked* on a holder or waste yarn and continue across row.

Next row: Purl.

Left Shoulder Shaping
Next row (RS): Knit to last 9 sts, w&t, purl back on WS.
Next row (RS): Knit to last 18 sts, w&t, purl back on WS.
Next row (RS): Knit to last 27 sts, w&t, purl back on WS.
Next row (RS): Knit to last 36 sts, w&t, purl back on WS.

Next row (RS): Knit, picking up wraps as you go. To pick up a wrap, place your needle under the wrap first, then knit it tog with the next st. Place all sts on a holder or waste yarn.

Right Shoulder Shaping
Join new yarn on WS at neck edge and work as follows:
Next row (WS): Purl to last 9 sts, w&t, knit back on RS.
Next row (WS): Purl to last 18 sts, w&t, knit back on RS.
Next row (WS): Purl to last 27 sts, w&t, knit back on RS.
Next row (WS): Purl to last 36 sts, w&t, knit back on RS.
Next row (WS): Purl across row, picking up wraps as you go. To pick up wraps, place the wrap on the left needle first, then purl it tog with the next st.

Place all sts on a holder or waste yarn.

FRONT
Place 136 front sts from holder onto needle.
Join yarn on RS and work in rows in St st until piece from armhole divide measures 4½ in / 11.5 cm. End having completed a WS row.

Neck Shaping
Next row (RS): Knit across 84 sts, place last 32 sts *just worked* on a holder or waste yarn for front neck, knit across last 52 sts.

Next row (WS): Purl to within 3 sts of end of row, p2togtbl (through back loop), p1.

Next row (RS): Knit.

Repeat last 2 rows 6 times more to 45 sts.

Purl one row.

Right Shoulder Shaping

Next row (RS): Knit across to last 9 sts, w&t, purl back on WS.

Next row (RS): Knit across to last 18 sts, w&t, purl back on WS.

Next row (RS): Knit across to last 27 sts, w&t, purl back on WS.

Next row (RS): Knit across to last 36 sts, w&t, purl back on WS.

Next row (RS): Knit across row, picking up wraps as you go. Place all sts on a holder or waste yarn.

Neck, Left Side, Shaping

Join new yarn on WS at neck edge and work as follows:

Next row (WS): P1, p2tog, purl to end.

Next row (RS): Knit.

Repeat last 2 rows 6 times more to 45 sts.

Knit 1 row.

Left Shoulder Shaping

Next row (WS): Purl across to last 9 sts, w&t, knit back on RS.

Next row (WS): Purl across to last 18 sts, w&t, knit back on RS.

Next row (WS): Purl across to last 27 sts, w&t, knit back on RS.

Next row (WS): Purl across to last 36 sts, w&t, knit back on RS.

Next row (WS): Purl across row, picking up wraps as you go.

Use the three-needle bind-off to connect shoulders together from the WS.

COLLAR

With 16 in / 40 cm circular needle, join yarn at back neck and knit 46 sts from holder, pick up and knit 19 sts to front center, knit 32 sts off holder at front, then 19 sts to back. [116 sts]

[K2, p2] rib until collar measures 9 in / 23 cm (or desired length). Bind off loosely in rib.

SLEEVES

Begin at underarm with 16 in / 40 cm circular needle and pick up and knit 70 sts. Place marker at underarm.

To work a decrease rnd: K1, k2tog, knit to within 3 sts of end-of-rnd marker, ssk, k1.

Work a decrease rnd every 6th rnd 16 times total to 40 sts. (Change to double-pointed needles as necessary.) Continue with no further decreases until sleeve measures 14 in / 35.5 cm (or 3 in / 7.5 cm less than desired length).

Work [k1, p1] rib for 3 in / 7.5 cm.
Bind off loosely in rib.

Make other sleeve to match.

FINISHING

Weave in any loose ends. Either do not block, to keep the fluffy effect, or steam lightly for a flatter fabric or block according to directions on ball band.

Francesca's Cabled Sweater

Cabled, oversized, comfy, and cozy—wear this roomy sweater for a walk in the woods or top your favorite flannels on a cold winter weekend.

SIZES
Small (Medium, Large)
Sized to fit Juniors 3–5 (7–9) (11–15)
Instructions are written for size Small; all other sizes are in parentheses.

FINISHED MEASUREMENTS
Chest: 38 (43, 48) in / 96.5 (109, 122) cm
Length: 22½ (23, 24) in / 57 (58.5, 61) cm

YARN
Cascade 220 Superwash; 3.5 oz / 100 g each approx. 220 yd / 200 m; 100% superwash wool
- 7 (8, 8) skeins #879 Very Berry

MATERIALS
- Size US 7 / 4.5 mm needles (*or size to obtain gauge*)
- Size US 5 / 3.25 mm needles
- Size US 5 / 3.25 mm 16 in / 40 cm circular needle
- Tapestry needle
- Waste yarn
- Pin-type markers
- Ring-type markers
- Row counter (optional, but helpful)

GAUGE
20 sts and 26 rows to 4 in / 10 cm in St st on size US 7 / 4.5 mm needles

STITCH GUIDE
C3F. Slip next 2 sts onto CN and hold at front, k1, then k2 from CN.
C3B. Slip next st onto CN and hold at back, k2, then k1 from CN.

C4F. Slip next 2 sts onto CN and hold at front, k2, then k2 from CN.

C4B. Slip next 2 sts onto CN and hold at back, k2, then k2 from CN.

C5B. Slip next 3 sts onto CN and hold at back, k2, place last st from CN back on left needle and knit it, then k2 from CN.

C6F. Slip next 3 sts onto CN and hold at front, k3, then k3 from CN.

C6B. Slip next 3 sts onto CN and hold at back, k3, then k3 from CN.

T3F. Slip next 2 sts onto CN and hold at front, p1, then k2 from CN.

T3B. Slip next 2 sts onto CN and hold at back, p1, then k2 from CN.

T5L. Slip next 3 sts onto CN and hold at front, k2, place last st from CN back on left needle and purl it, then k2 from CN.

Three-needle bind-off. Turn pieces inside out and place live stitches on 2 parallel needles. Then knit 2 stitches together, one from each of the parallel needles. Knit another 2 stitches together, one from each needle. You now have 2 stitches on your right needle; use your left needle to pull the first stitch over the second and off the needle (one stitch bound off). Continue binding off in this manner (k2tog, bind off 1).

STITCH PATTERNS

Twisted Rib
Row 1 (RS): [K2b, p2b] across, end with k2b.
Row 2 (WS): [P2b, k2b] across, end with p2b.
Repeat these 2 rows for pattern.

Seed Stitch
Row 1 (RS): [K1, p1] across, knit last st (if applicable).
Row 2 (WS): Purl the knits and knit the purls.
Repeat these 2 rows for pattern.

Cable Pattern A (over 13 sts)
Row 1 (RS): P3, C3B, p1, C3F, p3.
Row 2: K3, p3, k1, p3, k3.
Row 3: P2, C3B, p1, k1, p1, C3F, p2.
Row 4: K2, p3, k1, p1, k1, p3, k2.
Row 5: P1, C3B, p1, [k1, p1] twice, C3F, p1.
Row 6: K1, p3, [k1, p1] 3 times, p2, k1.
Row 7: C3B, p1, [k1, p1] 3 times, C3F.
Row 8: P3, k1, [p1, k1] 3 times, p3.
Row 9: K2, p1, [k1, p1] 4 times, k2.
Row 10: P2, k1, [p1, k1] 4 times, p2.
Row 11: T3F, p1, [k1, p1] 3 times, T3B.
Row 12: K1, p2, k1, [p1, k1] 3 times, p2, k1.
Row 13: P1, T3F, p1, [k1, p1] twice, T3B, p1
Row 14: K2, p2, k1, [p1, k1] twice, p2, k2.
Row 15: P2, T3F, p1, k1, p1, T3B, p2.
Row 16: K3, p2, k1, p1, k1, p2, k3.
Row 17: P3, T3F, p1, T3B, p3.
Row 18: K4, p2, k1, p2, k4.
Row 19: P4, C5B, p4
Row 20: K4, p5, k4.
Repeat these 20 rows for pattern.

Cable Pattern B (over 12 sts)
Row 1 (RS): K12.
Row 2: P12
Row 3: C6B, C6F.
Row 4: P12.
Row 5–8: Repeat rows 1 and 2 twice.
Rows 9 and 10: As rows 3 and 4.
Rows 11–14: Repeat rows 1 and 2 twice.
Row 15: C6F, C6B.
Row 16: P12.
Rows 17–20: Repeat rows 1 and 2 twice.
Rows 21 and 22: As row 15 and 16.
Rows 23 and 24: As rows 1 and 2.
Repeat these 24 rows for pattern.

Cable Pattern C (over 15 sts)
Row 1 (RS): P5, T5L, p5.
Row 2: K5, p2, k1, p2, k5.
Row 3: P4, T3B, k1, T3F, p4.
Row 4: K4, p2, k1, p1, k1, p2 k4.
Row 5: P3, T3B, k1, p1, k1, T3F, p3.
Row 6: K3, p2, [k1, p1] twice, k1, p2, k3.
Row 7: P2, T3B, [k1, p1] twice, k1, T3F, p2.
Row 8: K2, p2, [k1, p1] 3 times, k1, p2, k2.
Row 9: P1, T3B, [k1, p1] 3 times, k1, T3F, p1.
Row 10: K1, p2, [k1, p1] 4 times, k1, p2, k1.
Row 11: T3B, [k1, p1] 4 times, k1, T3F.
Row 12: P2, [k1, p1] 5 times, k1, p2.
Repeat these 12 rows for pattern.

Center Cable Pattern D (over 20 sts)
Row 1 (RS): K6, C4B, C4F, k6.
Row 2 and all WS rows: Purl.
Row 3: K4, C4B, k4, C4F, k4.
Row 5: K2, C4B, k8, C4F, k2.
Row 7: C4B, k12, C4F.
Row 8: Purl.
Repeat these 8 rows

PATTERN NOTES

- Front and back worked separately.
- Sleeves picked up at shoulders and worked flat.
- Collar picked up after seaming and worked in the round.
- Cable pattern sequence for body = A, B, C, D, C, B, A, with 2 sts separating cables. Cables are color coded for ease in keeping your place. Markers help between cables. Once you get going, the cables are easy to read as you knit.
- Helpful hint: other than the seed st at the sides, all WS rows are *knit the knits* and *purl the purls*.

FRONT

With size US 5 / 3.25 mm needles, cast on 138 (150, 158) sts.
Row 1 (RS): [K2b, p2b] across, end with k2b.
Row 2 (WS): [P2b, k2b] across, end with p2b.
Work in twisted rib for 2 in / 5 cm (or desired length).
Change to size US 7 / 4.5 mm needles and work as follows:
Row 1 (RS): K2, seed st over next 9 (15, 19) sts, p2, p3, C3B, p1, C3F, p3, p2, k12, p2, p5, T5L, p5, p2, k6, C4B, C4F, k6, p2, p5, T5L, p5, p2, k12, p2, p3, C3B, p1, C3F, p3, p2, seed st over next 9 (15, 19) sts, k2.
Row 2 (WS): P2, seed st over next 9 (15, 19) sts, k2, k3, p3, k1, p3, k3, k2, p12, k2, k5, p2, k1, p2, k5, k2, p20, k2, k5, p2, k1, p2, k5, k2, p12, k2, k3, p3, k1, p3, k3, k2, seed st over next 9 (15, 19) sts, p2.
Row 3: K2, seed st over next 9 (15, 19) sts, p2, p2, C3B, p1, k1, p1, C3F, p2, p2, C6B, C6F, p2, p4, T3B, k1, T3F, p4, p2, k4, C4B, k4, C4F, k4, p2, p4, T3B, k1, T3F, p4, p2, C6B, C6F, p2, p2, C3B, p1, k1, p1, C3F, p2, p2, seed st over next 9 (15, 19) sts, k2.
Row 4: P2, seed st over next 9 (15, 19) sts, k2, k2, p3, k1, p1, k1, p3, k2, k2, p12, k2, p4, T3B, k1, T3F, p4, k2,

p20, k2, p4, T3B, k1, T3F, p4, k2, p12, k2, k2, p3, k1, p1, k1, p3, k2, k2, seed st over next 9 (15, 19) sts, p2.
These 4 rows set pattern. Continue working through rows of each cable as established until front measures 14 (14½, 15) in / 35.5 (37, 38) cm from beginning (or desired length to underarm). End having completed a WS row.

Armhole Shaping

Next row (RS): Bind off 6 sts, work across.
Next row (WS): Bind off 6 sts, work across to last 2 sts, p2.
To work a decrease row: K2, work 2 tog, work across in pattern as established to last 4 sts, work 2 tog, k2.
Next row (RS): Work a decrease row now and every RS row 2 (3, 4) times more to 120 (130, 136) sts. While keeping first and last 2 sts in St st, work pattern as established until armhole from bind-off measures 6 (6, 6½) in / 15 (15, 16.5) cm. End having completed a WS row.

Neck Shaping

Next row (RS): K2, work in pattern across 78 (82, 90) sts, place last 36 (42, 44) sts *just worked* on a holder or waste yarn for center neck, and continue across in pattern to last 2 sts, k2.

Next row (WS): Work in pattern to last 2 sts, p2.

To work a RS decrease row: K2, ssk, work in pattern to end.

Work a decrease row on next and every 4th row 4 times total until 38 (40, 42) sts remain. Continue if necessary until armhole measures 8½ (8½, 9) in / 21.5 (21.5, 23) cm.

Place sts on a holder or waste yarn and complete other side as follows:

Join new yarn at neck edge on WS and p2, work to end.

To work a RS decrease row: Work across in pattern to last 4 sts, k2tog, k2.

Work a decrease on next and every 4th row 4 times total until 38 (40, 42) sts remain. Continue if necessary until armhole measures 8½ (8½, 9) in / 21.5 (21.5, 23) cm. Place sts on a holder or waste yarn.

BACK

Work same as for front until piece from armhole bind-off measures 7½ (7½, 8) in / 19 (19, 20.5) cm (or 1 in / 2.5 cm less than total front length). End having completed a WS row.

Neck Shaping

Next row (RS): K2, work in pattern across 78 (82, 90) sts, place last 36 (42, 44) sts *just worked* on a holder or waste yarn for center neck, and continue across in pattern to last 2 sts, k2.

Next row (WS): Work in pattern to last 2 sts, p2.

To work a RS decrease row: K2, ssk, work in pattern to end.

Work a decrease on next, and *every RS row* 4 times total until 38 (40, 42) sts remain. Continue if necessary until armhole measures 8½ (8½, 9) in / 21.5 (21.5, 23) cm.

Place sts on a holder or waste yarn and complete other side as follows:

Join new yarn at neck edge on WS and p2, work to end.

To work a RS decrease row: Work across in pattern to last 4 sts, k2tog, k2.

Work a decrease on next and *every RS row* 4 times total until 38 (40, 42) sts remain. Continue if necessary until armhole measures 8½ (8½, 9) in / 21.5 (21.5, 23) cm.

Use the three-needle bind-off to connect shoulder sts from the WS.

SLEEVES

Note: Sleeve pattern omits cable C. Sequence is Seed st, B, A, D, A, B, Seed st.

With size US 7 / 4.5 mm needles, from RS at bind-off, pick up and knit through 6 bound-off sts; 54 (54, 57) sts to shoulder; 54 (54, 57) sts to other bind-off; then 6 sts through bind-off. [120 (120, 126) sts]

To work a decrease on a RS row: K2, ssk, work in pattern to last 4 sts, k2tog, k2.

To work a decrease on a WS row: P2, p2tog, work in pattern to last 4 sts, p2togtbl (through back loop), p2.

Note: The set-up row and first 5 rows will decrease away the 12 bound-off sts at underarms to eliminate bulk.

Set-up row (WS, decrease row): P2, p2tog, [k1, p1] seed st over next 15 (15, 18) sts, place a marker, k2, p12, k2, k3, p3, k1, p3, k3, k2, p20, k2, k3, p3, k1, p3, k3, k2, p12, k2, place a marker, [p1, k1] seed st over 15 (15, 18) sts to last 4 sts, p2togtbl (through back loop), p2.

Row 1 (RS, decrease row): K2, ssk, seed st over next 14 (14, 17) sts, slip marker, p2, k12, p2, p3, C3B, p1, C3F, p3, p2, k6, C4B, C4F, k6, p2, p3, C3B, p1, C3F, p3, p2, k12, p2, slip marker, seed st over next 14 (14, 17) sts to last 4 sts, k2tog, k2.

Row 2 (decrease row): P2, p2tog, seed st over next 13 (13, 16) sts, knit the knits and purl the purls over cable patterns, seed st over 13 (13, 16) sts to last 4 sts, p2togtbl (through back loop), p2.

Row 3 (decrease row): K2, ssk, seed st over next 12 (12, 15) sts, p2, C6B, C6F, p2, p2, C3B, p1, k1, p1, C3F, p2, p2, k4, C4B, k4, C4F, k4, p2, p2, C3B, p1, k1, p1, C3F, p2, p2, C6B, C6F, p2, seed st over 12 (12, 15) sts to last 4 sts, k2tog, k2.

Row 4 (decrease row): P2, p2tog, seed st over next 11 (11, 14) sts, knit the knits and purl the purls over cable patterns, seed st over 13 (13, 16) sts to last 4 sts, p2togtbl (through back loop), p2.

Row 5 (decrease row): K2, ssk, seed st over next 10 (10, 14) sts, p2, k12, p2, p1, C3B, p1, [k1, p1] twice, C3F, p1, p2, k2, C4B, k8, C4F, k2, p2, p1, C3B, p1, [k1, p1] twice, C3F, p1, p2, k12, p2, seed st over 12 (12, 15) sts, to last 4 sts, k2tog, k2. [108 (108, 114) sts remain.]

Continue in pattern as established and, *at the same time*, work a decrease row every 3rd row 27 (27, 30) times times until 54 sts remain. Continue if necessary until sleeve measures 15 in / 38 cm from underarm (or desired length minus length of cuff). End having completed a RS row.

(WS): Change to size US 5 / 3.25 mm needles and work [p2b, k2b]. Work twisted rib for 2 in / 5 cm (or desired length). Bind off loosely on RS in [k2, p2] rib. Sew up side and sleeve seams using a mattress stitch from the RS.

Make other sleeve to match.

COLLAR

With 16 in / 40 cm size US 5 / 3.25 mm circular needle, knit across 36 (42, 44) back sts, pick up and knit 26 (24, 24) sts to front center, knit across 36 (42, 44) front sts, pick up and knit 26 (24, 24) sts. [124 (132, 136) sts] Make sure number is a multiple of 4. Place a marker and work [k2b, p2b] twisted rib for 2 in / 5 cm (or desired length). Bind off loosely in [k2, p2] rib.

FINISHING

Weave in any ends and steam lightly, or block according to directions on ball band.

Jade Top

Sleek ribs adorn this lightweight, long-sleeved top, which you can wear off the shoulder or on.

SIZES
Juniors 3 (5, 7, 9) (11, 13, 15)
*Instructions are written for size 3; all other sizes are in
  parentheses.*

FINISHED MEASUREMENTS
Chest: 29 (32, 34, 35) (35½, 36, 38) in / 73.5 (81.5, 86.5,
  89) (90, 91.5, 96.5) cm
Waist: 24 (24½, 25, 27) (28½, 30, 32) in / 61 (62, 63.5,
  68.5) (72.5, 76, 81.5) cm
Sleeve length to underarm: 16½ (17, 17½, 17½) (17½, 18,
  18) in / 42 (43, 44.5, 44.5) 44.5, 45.5, 45.5) cm

YARN
Cascade Heritage Yarn; 3.5 oz / 100 g each approx.
  437 yd / 400 meters; 75% superwash merino, 25%
  nylon
  • 4 (4, 4, 4) (5, 5, 5) skeins #5627 Jade

MATERIALS
  • Size US 1 / 2.25 mm 24 in / 60 cm circular needle
    (*or size to obtain gauge*)
  • Size US 1 / 2.25 mm 36 in / 91.5 cm circular needle
    (this length needed when sleeves are joined with
    body)
  • Size US 1 / 2.25 mm double-pointed needles
  • Extra 24 in / 60 cm circular needle for holding body
    sts while knitting sleeves (optional)
  • Waste yarn
  • Ring-type markers, two colors
  • Tapestry needle
  • Thin cable needle (or size US 1 / 2.25 mm sock
    needle)

GAUGE

52 sts and 48 rows to 4 in / 10 cm in 2x2 rib, slightly stretched

36 sts of 4x4 rib = 3½ in / 9 cm, slightly stretched

STITCH GUIDE

M1K. Insert left needle into the horozontal bar that lies between last st worked and next st from the front, then knit into the back of it.

M1P. Insert left needle into the horozontal bar that lies between last st worked and next st from the front, then purl into the back of it.

PATTERN NOTES

- Pattern worked in the round from the bottom up with seaming at underarms.
- Sleeves are worked separately in the round, then joined at yoke.
- Please don't be over-concerned with numbers. I give them so the rib pattern will line up at first and for placement of the 4x4 rib at center front, but as you increase and decrease at the sides, it's okay to be off a few sts as this pattern has lots of stretchy give and miscounts won't change the fit.
- The front and back stitch counts are not the same because the 4x4 rib pattern on the front has a slightly different gauge.

BODY

With 24 in / 60 cm circular needle, cast on 340 (356, 364, 372) (388, 404, 420) sts. Place a marker and join into a round, being careful not to twist sts.

Rnd 1: [K2, p2] 22 (23, 23, 24) (25, 26, 27) times, place different color side marker, [k2, p2] 16 (17, 18, 18) (19, 20, 21) times, [k4, p4] 4 times, k4 (this is the center front), [p2, k2] 16 (17, 18, 18) (19, 20, 21) times, place other side marker, [p2, k2] 22 (23, 23, 24) (25, 26, 27) times (yes, there will be a decorative k4 at center back).

Work as established (knit the knits and purl the purls) until piece from beginning measures 1 in / 2.5 cm.

Begin decreases for waist shaping as follows:

To work a decrease rnd: Work to within 2 sts of side marker, p2tog, slip marker, k2tog, work to within 2

sts of other side marker, k2tog, slip marker, p2tog, continue to end of round marker. [4 sts decreased]

Note: As the pattern changes, not every decrease rnd will read the same; just work 2 sts together before and after each side marker, keeping rib pattern as close as possible.

Work a decrease rnd every 9th round 7 times to 162 (170, 170, 178) (186, 194, 202) sts on the back and 150 (158, 166, 166) (174, 182, 190) sts on the front.

Work with no further decreases until piece from beginning measures 6 in / 15 cm (or desired length to waist).

Waist to Bust Shaping

Note: Increase rnds will add a stitch on each side of side markers (4 sts per rnd). Do your best to incorporate them into rib pattern using either a M1, kfb, pfb, or any method to increase a stitch on either side of the side markers and keep the rib pattern going as best you can.

Work an increase round every 8th (8th, 9th, 10th) (8th, 6th, 6th) round 7 (7, 7, 7) (10, 13, 13) times to 176 (184, 184, 192) (206, 220, 228) sts on the back and 164 (172, 180, 180) (194, 208, 216) sts on the front.

Work with no further increases until piece from the beginning measures 11 (11, 11½, 12) (12½, 12½, 13) in / 28 (28, 29, 30.5) (32, 32, 33) cm (or desired length to underarm, snug into armpit).

Place all sts on a spare needle or waste yarn and hold for later.

SLEEVES

With double-pointed needles (or preferred method of working in the round) cast on 76 sts (all sizes). Place marker (at underarm) and join into a round, being careful not to twist sts.

Rnd 1: [K2, p2] 7 times, [k4, p4] twice, k4, [p2, k2] 7 times. (Yes, there will be a k4 at the center under-arm.)

Continue as established (knit the knits and purl the purls) for 1 in / 2.5 cm.

First increase rnd: K2, M1P, work in pattern to within 2 sts of marker, M1P, k2. [2 sts increased]

Work 5 rounds.

Second increase rnd: Work same as first. (You will have 4 purls together before and after the k4 at center underarm.)

Work 5 rounds.

Third increase rnd: K2, p2, M1K, p2, continue around to within 4 sts of marker, M1K, p2, k2.

Work 5 rounds.

Fourth increase rnd: Work same as second.

(These 4 increase rounds set rib pattern as the sleeve increases in width.)

Work an appropriate increase round every 6th round 28 (28, 28, 28) (34, 34, 34) times total, incorporating increases as described above to keep the rib pattern consistent.

On next round, adjust (if necessary) to 132 (132, 132, 132) (132, 144, 144) sts. Work with no further increases until sleeve measures 16½ (17, 17½, 17½) (17½, 18, 18) in / 42 (43, 44.5, 44.5) (44.5, 45.5, 45.5) cm (or

desired length to underarm, snug into armpit). On last round, bind off 16 sts before and after beg-of-rnd marker (32 sts bound-off total). Place remaining sts on a holder or waste yarn.

Make other sleeve to match.

Join Sleeves and Body

Begin at center-back marker and work to within 16 sts of side marker; bind off 16, remove side marker, and bind off 16 more. Place marker, drop yarn, and slip 100 (100, 100, 100) (100, 112, 112) sts from sleeve onto right needle, place marker, work across front sts to within 16 sts of other side marker, bind off 16 sts. Remove side marker and bind off 16 more, place marker, slip 100 (100, 100, 100) (100, 112, 112) sts from other sleeve onto right needle, place marker, and work remaining back sts to beginning of round marker. [476 (490, 500, 508) (536, 588, 604) sts total]

Work 3 rounds, with 4 knits remaining at center back, adjusting rib to work out with [p2, k2] before each raglan marker and [k2, p2] after each raglan marker. (You might have to work knits over purls at the sleeve-join areas on the first round, then decrease away a few stitches to make the rib pattern work

on the next 2 rounds. *It's important to have the ribs lined up at the markers for the decorative decreases of the raglan shaping to follow.*)

Begin Raglan Shaping

Rnd 1 (decrease rnd): *Work to within 10 sts of raglan marker, slip next 2 sts onto CN and hold at front, p2tog, knit 2 from CN, k2, [p2, k2, slip marker, k2, p2], k2, place next 2 sts onto CN and hold at back, k2, p2tog from CN, repeat from * around. [8 sts decreased]

Rnd 2 and all even rnds: Knit the knits and purl the purls.

Rnd 3 (decrease rnd): *Work to within 8 sts of raglan marker, slip next 2 sts to CN and hold at front, p2tog, k2 from CN, [p2, k2, slip marker, k2, p2], place next 2 sts to CN and hold at back, k2, p2tog from CN, repeat from * around. [8 sts decreased]

Rnd 5 (decrease rnd): *Work to within 8 sts of raglan marker, p2tog, k2, [p2, k2, slip marker, k2, p2], k2, p2tog (continue rib pattern as established), repeat from * around. [8 sts decreased]

Rnd 7 (decrease round): Work same as for rnd 5.

Rnd 8: Knit the knits and purl the purls.

Repeat rnds 1–8, working a decrease round every other round until raglan seam from underarm bind-off measures approx. 3½ (3½, 4, 4½) (4½, 5, 5) in / 9 (9, 10, 11.5) (11.5, 13, 13) cm.

Knit 2 rounds, if desired, for decorative detail to distinguish between body and collar.

COLLAR

Resume rib pattern and continue with decreases until raglan seam measures 5½ (5½, 6, 6½) (6½, 7, 7) in / 14 (14, 15, 16.5) (16.5, 18, 18) cm or desired length. Bind off loosely in rib.

FINISHING

Stitch armholes to body at underarm. Weave in any loose ends and steam lightly, or block according to directions on ball band.

Open-Back Sweater

An easy, ribbed, one-piece, no-fuss knit, this sweater is stretchy and oversized with an open-back detail.

SIZES
Juniors Small (Medium, Large)
Sized to fit Juniors 0–3 (5–9) (11–15)
Instructions are written for size Small; all other sizes are in parentheses.

FINISHED MEASUREMENTS
Chest: 38 (42, 46) in / 96.5 (106.5, 117) cm
Length: 20 (22, 24) in / 51 (56, 61) cm

YARN
Cascade 220 Superwash; 3.5 oz / 100 g each approx.
220 yd / 200 m; 100% superwash wool
  • 4 (5, 5) skeins #880 Marionberry
Cascade Heritage Wave; 3.5 oz / 100 g each approx.
437 yd / 400 m; 75% superwash merino, 25% nylon
  • 3 skeins (all sizes) #507 Lava

MATERIALS
  • Size US 10.5 / 6.5 mm 24 in / 60 cm circular needle
    (*or size to obtain gauge*)
  • Size US 9 /5.5 mm needles for back tab and sleeve
    cuffs
  • Tapestry needle
  • Waste yarn
  • Pin-type markers

GAUGE
18 sts and 18 rows to 4 in / 10 cm on size US 10.5 /
  6.5 mm needles in [k1, p1] rib with 2 strands held
  together

STITCH GUIDE

Yf. Yarn forward; move the yarn in front of the working needle as if to purl.

W&t. Wrap and turn; slip the next stitch, bring the yarn to the front (or back if a purl row), then put the stitch back on the left needle, turn and work back across next row. Some stitches will be left unworked.

PATTERN NOTES

- Entire garment is made with one strand of Cascade 220 Superwash and one strand of Cascade Wave held together.
- Front and back are worked as one piece, with division for neck shaping and V-shaped back.
- Sleeves are picked up and knit flat from shoulders.
- Since the pattern will look the same on both sides, marking the RS tells you which side to leave ends

to tuck and keeps a knit st on the RS edge for easier seaming.

- To pick up wraps on a purl st, place wrap on left needle and purl it together with st on needle.
- To pick up wrap on a knit st, insert needle under wrap first, then knit it together with st on needle.

FRONT

With two strands held together, cast on 90 (95, 103) sts. Work in [k1, p1] rib (mark this as right side) for 17 (19, 20) in / 43 (48.5, 51) cm. End having completed a WS row.

Front Neck Shaping

Next row (RS): Work across 30 (32, 35) sts, bind off (in pattern) next 30 (31, 33) sts for center front, continue to end of row. Place first 30 (32, 35) sts on a holder or waste yarn.

Next row (WS): Work to last 2 sts, work 2 together.

Next row (RS): Work across.

Repeat last 2 rows 2 times more (3 sts total decreased) to 27 (29, 32) sts.

Continue working on these sts only until piece measures 2½ in / 6.5 cm from center bind-off. End having completed a WS row.

Note: Mark outside edge stitch (with hanging pin) as center shoulder for ease in placement of sleeves; this is very important for measuring later.

Continue shoulder shaping as follows:

(RS): Work to last 8 sts, w&t, work back on WS.

Next row (RS): Work to last 16 sts, w&t, work back on WS.

Next row (RS): Work across all sts, picking up wraps by working them tog with st on needle.

Work one WS row. This completes the front.

Work back shoulder shaping as follows:

(RS): Work to last 8 sts, w&t, work back on WS.

Next row (RS): Work to last 16 sts, w&t, work back on WS.

Next row (RS): Work across all sts, picking up wraps. Shoulder shaping complete. Hang another pin-type marker at *neck* edge (very important for placement of joining tab at back)

BACK

Note: All increases are worked 1 st in from neck edge, throwing rib pattern off for a few rows, but don't worry. Keep knits over knits and purls over purls.

To work an increase row on RS: Work first stitch, M1, work in rib across.

To work an increase row on WS: Work in rib across to last st, M1, work last st.

Begin on WS and work an increase row every 3rd row 18 (19, 20) times total to 45 (48, 52) sts. Cut yarn and place sts on a holder or waste yarn.

Complete other shoulder as follows:

Place 30 (32, 35) held sts for right shoulder on needle, join new yarn at neck edge.

(WS): Work 2tog, work to end.

Next row (RS): Work as established.

Repeat last 2 rows 2 times more to 27 (29, 32) sts.

Continue working on these sts until piece measures 2 in / 5 cm from center bind-off. End having completed a RS row. *Mark outside edge stitch with hanging pin as center shoulder for ease in placement of sleeves; this is very important for measuring later.*

Continue shoulder shaping as follows:

(WS): Work to last 8 sts, w&t, work back on RS.

Next row (WS): Work to last 16 sts, w&t, work back on RS.

Next row (WS): Work across all sts, picking up wraps by working them tog with st on needle.

Work one RS row. This completes the front.

Work back shoulder shaping as follows:

(WS): Work to last 8 sts, w&t, work back on RS.

Next row (WS): Work to last 16 sts, w&t, work back on RS.

Next row (WS): Work across all sts picking up wraps. Shoulder shaping complete. Hang another pin-type marker at *neck* edge (very important for placement of joining tab).

Continue on RS as row 1 and work an increase row every 3rd row (1 st in from neck edge, same as for other side of back) 18 (19, 20) times total, to 45 (48, 52) sts. End having completed a WS row.

Join Backs

Work across, place sts from other back holder. On Medium and Large sizes, work 2 tog at join and continue across row. You should have the original cast-on of 90 (95, 103) sts.

Work in pattern until back measures same as front. Bind off in rib.

SLEEVES

At outside edge, using center-shoulder marker as a guide, measure and mark 6½ in / 16.5 cm down on front and same distance on back. With two strands held together, join yarn on RS at marker and pick up and knit 32 sts to center shoulder, 1 st at shoulder marker, and 32 sts to other marker. [65 sts]

Begin on a WS row with a purl st and work in 1x1 rib across to last st, end p1.

Next row (RS): [K1, p1] across to last st, k1.

To work a decrease row on RS: K1, k2tog, continue in rib to last 3 sts, k2tog, k1.

To work a decrease row on WS: P1, p2tog, work in rib across to last 3 sts, p2tog, p1.

Work a decrease row every 5th row 14 times to 37 sts.

Change to size US 9 / 5.5 mm needles and work with no further decreases until sleeve measures 16 (17, 18) in / 40.5 (43, 45.5) cm or desired length. Bind off in pattern.

Make other sleeve to match.

BACK JOINING TAB

Note: This piece holds the backs together at the neck, keeping the sweater from falling off the shoulders, and will be turned sideways and stitched on at neck edge markers.

With size US 9 / 5.5 mm needles, cast on 11 sts, leaving a 9 in / 23 cm tail for seaming. Work in [k1, p1] rib until piece measures 2 in / 5 cm. Bind off in rib, leaving a 9 in / 23 cm tail for seaming.

Turn back tab sideways and close back neck by stitching tab under both backs at neck markers.

FINISHING

Stitch side and sleeve seams from the RS with a mattress stitch, and weave in any ends.

Sweater can be worn as is, or stretched out to any width by steaming lightly while pulling on fabric.

Pretty in Pink

This sleeveless little top sports a braided cable detail. Wear it casual or dress it up.

SIZES
Juniors 3 (5, 7, 9) (11, 13, 15)
Instructions are written for size 3; all other sizes are in parentheses.

FINISHED MEASUREMENTS
Chest: 29 (32, 34, 35) (35½, 36, 38) in / 73.5 (81.5, 86.5, 89) (90, 91.5, 96.5) cm
Waist: 24 (24½, 25, 27) (28½, 30, 32) in / 61 (62, 63.5, 68.5) (72.5, 76, 81.5) cm
Total length: 18 (18½, 19, 19½) (20, 21, 21½) in / 45.5 (47, 48.5, 49.5) (51, 53.5, 54.5) cm

YARN
Cascade Heritage Silk; 3.5 oz / 100 g each approx. 437 yd / 400 meters; 85% superwash merino, 15% silk
- 2 skeins #5718 Gossamer Pink

MATERIALS
- Size US 3 / 3.25 mm 24 in / 60 cm circular needle (*or size to obtain gauge*)
- Size US 3 / 3.25 mm 16 in / 40 cm circular needle
- Cable needle
- Tapestry needle
- Waste yarn
- Ring-type marker

GAUGE

28 sts and 38 rows to 4 in / 10 cm in St st

STITCH GUIDE

C4B. Slip next 2 sts onto CN and hold at back, k2, then k2 from CN.

C4F. Slip next 2 sts to CN and hold at front, k2, then k2 from CN.

STITCH PATTERNS

Braid Cable in *Rows* over 6 sts

Row 1 (RS): K2, C4F.

Row 2: P6.

Row 3: C4B, K2.

Row 4: P6.

Braid Cable in *Rounds* over 6 sts

Rnd 1 (RS): K2, C4F.

Rnd 2: K6.

Rnd 3: C4B, k2.

Rnd 4: K6.

PATTERN NOTES

- Worked in the round to armhole shaping, then front and back worked separately.

BODY

With 24 in / 60 cm needle, cast on 176 (176, 180, 192) (200, 212, 224) sts. Place a marker and join into a round, being careful not to twist sts.

Work [k2, p2] rib for 3 in / 7.5 cm (or desired length).

Change to St st and knit 88 (88, 90, 96) (100, 106, 112) sts, place side marker, knit to beg of round.

To work an increase rnd: K2, M1, knit to within 2 sts of side marker, M1, k2, slip marker, k2, M1, knit to within 2 sts of end-of-round marker, M1, k2. [4 sts increased per round]

Work an increase round every 6th (4th, 4th, 5th) (5th, 6th, 6th) round 9 (12, 14, 13) (12, 10, 11) times total, to 212 (224, 236, 244) (248, 252, 268) sts. Work even (if necessary) until work from beginning measures 9 (9, 10, 10½) (10½, 11, 11½) in / 23 (23, 25.5, 26.5) (26.5, 28, 29) cm (or desired length to underarm).

Divide Front and Back

Knit 106 (112, 118, 122) (124, 126, 134) sts. Place remaining sts on a holder or waste yarn for front.

Back

Purl one WS row.

Raglan Armhole Shaping

Bind off 2 (3, 3, 3) (3, 4, 6) sts at beg of next 2 rows. [102 (106, 112, 116) (118, 118, 122) sts remain.]

Row 1 (RS): K2, p1, k2, C4F, p1, k1, ssk, knit to last 13 sts, k2tog, k1, p1, k2, C4F, p1, k2.

Row 2 (WS): K1, p1, k1, p6, k1, purl to last 10 sts, k1, p6, k1, p1, k1.

Row 3: K2, p1, C4B, k2, p1, k1, ssk, knit to last 13 sts, k2tog, k1, p1, C4B, k2, p1, k2.

Row 4: Same as row 2.

These 4 rows set the Braid Cable pattern and raglan decreases.

Continue in this manner until 34 (34, 38, 38) (42, 42, 42) sts remain. (At any time, should your raglan armhole become long enough, stop at 42 sts and continue with directions for the largest size.)

End having completed a WS row. (Keep track of which WS row for collar.)

FRONT

Place sts from holder or waste yarn on needle, join new yarn and work same as for back.

COLLAR

Note: For the collar, you will be working the Braid Cable in *rounds*.

With 16 in / 40 cm circular needle, find proper row (1 or 3) and work across RS of front as follows:

Next row (RS): *K2, p1, work 6 sts of Braid Cable, p1, k2, [p2, k2] 2 (2, 2, 3) (3, 3, 4) times, p2, k2, p1, work 6 sts of Braid Cable, p1, k2, cast on 30 (30, 26, 26) (22, 22, 22) sts, repeat from * once more. [128 sts, all sizes]

Next rnd: Work pattern sts as established, and 2x2 rib over all others until collar measures 2½ in / 6.5 cm (or desired length). Bind off *loosely* in pattern, working a k2tog over center 2 sts of a C4B and an ssk over center 2 sts of a C4F (if applicable).

FINISHING

At each underarm, use a small length of yarn and tapestry needle to stitch bind-off sts together and tidy underarms. Weave in any ends and steam lightly, or block according to directions on ball band.

Sarasota V-Neck Shirt

Casual, comfortable, and roomy, this oversized seed stitch top with low back bottom and higher neck front will look good on all junior shapes and sizes. Optional stylish straps add detail at the front neck.

SIZES
One size looks good on all Juniors

FINISHED MEASUREMENTS
Chest: 46 in / 117 cm
Length: 25 in / 63.5 cm

YARN
Cascade Sarasota; 3.5 oz / 100 g each approx. 314 yd / 287.5 m; 60% cotton, 40% acrylic
- 5 skeins #10 Silver

MATERIALS
- Size US 5 / 3.75 mm needles (*or size to obtain gauge*)
- Tapestry needle
- Waste yarn
- Pin-type markers
- Ring-type markers

GAUGE
20 sts and 36 rows to 4 in / 10 cm in seed st

STITCH GUIDE
Seed2tog. Keeping the seed stitch pattern correct, knit or purl the next two sts together.
Three-needle bind-off. Turn pieces WS or RS together, as desired, and place live stitches on 2 parallel needles. Then knit 2 stitches together, one from each of the parallel needles. Knit another 2 stitches together, one from each needle. You now have 2 stitches on your right needle; use your left needle to pull the first stitch over the second and off the needle (one stitch bound off). Continue binding off in this manner (k2tog, bind off 1).

W&t. Wrap and turn; slip the next st, bring the yarn to the front (or back if a purl st), then put the st back on the left needle, turn and work back across next row, leaving some sts unworked. To pick up a wrap on a knit st, insert needle under the wrap first and knit it tog with st on needle. To pick up a wrap on a purl st, pick up the wrap from behind, place it on left needle and purl it tog with st.

STITCH PATTERN

Seed Stitch
Row 1: [K1, p1] repeat across.
Row 2: Knit the purls and purl the knits.
Repeat row 2 for pattern.

PATTERN NOTES

- Front and back worked separately, sleeves picked up and knit flat from shoulders. Decorative front strips optional.
- Two sts will remain in St st at both sides for decorative border and ease in sewing side seams. All other sts will be worked in seed st.

BACK

Cast on 47 sts, place marker, cast on 17 sts, place marker, cast on 47 sts. (17 sts at center back will not be used in the wrap and turns, and the markers are for reference only.) [115 sts total]
Next row (WS): P2, [k1, p1] across to last 3 sts, k1, p2.
Next row (RS): K2, *Seed st to last 7 sts, w&t, repeat from * once.
Next row (RS): *Seed st to last 12 sts, w&t, repeat from * once.
Next row (RS): *Seed st to last 17 sts, w&t, repeat from * once.
Next row (RS): *Seed st to last 22 sts, w&t, repeat from * once.
Next row (RS): *Seed st to last 27 sts, w&t, repeat from * once.
Next row (RS): *Seed st to last 32 sts, w&t, repeat from * once.
Next row (RS): *Seed st to last 37 sts, w&t, repeat from * once.
Next row (RS): Seed st to last 42 sts, w&t, work across row, removing center markers, and picking up wraps as you come to them to last 2 sts, p2.

Next row (RS): K2, seed st across to last 2 sts, k2.
Lower back shaping is now complete.
Continue working in St st on the 2 sts at beg and end of every row, with all others in seed st until piece from beginning measures (from side edge) 24½ in / 62 cm. End having completed a WS row.
Next row (RS): K2, work 33 sts in seed st, k2, k41 (for back neck), k2, work 33 sts in seed st, k2.
Next row (WS): P2, work 33 sts in seed st, p2, p 41, p2, work 33 sts in seed st, p2.

Back Neck Shaping

Next row (RS): K2, work 33 sts in seed st, k2, bind off center 41 sts, k2, work seed st to last 2 sts, k2.

Left Shoulder Shaping

Next row (WS): P2, work seed st to last 2 sts, p2.

Next row (RS): K2, work seed st to within 10 sts of end, w&t, work seed st back to last 2 sts, p2.

Next row (RS): K2, work seed st to within 20 sts of end, w&t, work seed st back to last 2 sts, p2.

Next row (RS): K2, work seed st to within 30 sts of end, w&t, work seed st back to last 2 sts, p2.

Next row (RS): Knit.

Next row (WS): Purl.

Place sts on a holder or waste yarn.

Right Shoulder Shaping

Join new yarn at neck edge on WS, p2, work seed st across to last 10 sts, w&t, work seed st back to last 2 sts, k2.

Next row (WS): P2, work seed st to within 20 sts of end, w&t, work seed st back to last 2 sts, k2.

Next row (WS): P2, work seed st to within 30 sts of end, w&t, work seed st back to last 2 sts, k2.

Next row (WS): Purl across.

Next row (RS): Knit. Place sts on a holder or waste yarn.

FRONT

Cast on 47 sts, place marker, cast on 17 sts, place marker, cast on 47 sts. (17 sts at center front will not be used in the wrap and turns, but markers are needed for reference.) [115 sts total]

Row 1 (WS): P2, work 40 sts in seed st, w&t, work seed st back to last 2 sts, k2.

Next row (WS): P2, work 35 sts in seed st, w&t, work seed st to last 2 sts, k2.

Next row (WS): P2, work 30 sts in seed st, w&t, work seed st to last 2 sts, k2.

Next row (WS): P2, work 25 sts in seed st, w&t, work seed st to last 2 sts, k2.

Next row (WS): P2, work 20 sts in seed st, w&t, work seed st to last 2 sts, k2.

Next row (WS): P2, work 15 sts in seed st, w&t, work seed st to last 2 sts, k2.

Next row (WS): P2, work 10 sts in seed st, w&t, work seed st to last 2 sts, k2.

Next row (WS): P2, work 5 sts in seed st, w&t, work seed st to last 2 sts, k2.

Next row (WS): P2, work seed st across (leave markers in place) to within 2 sts of end of row, p2.

Next row (RS): K2, work 40 sts in seed st, w&t, work seed st to last 2 sts, p2.

Next row (RS): K2, work 35 sts in seed st, w&t, work seed st to last 2 sts, p2.

Next row (RS): K2, work 30 sts in seed st, w&t, work seed st to last 2 sts, p2.

Next row (RS): K2, work 25 sts in seed st, w&t, work seed st to last 2 sts, p2.

Next row (RS): K2, work 20 sts in seed st, w&t, work seed st to last 2 sts, p2.

Next row (RS): K2, work 15 sts in seed st, w&t, work seed st to last 2 sts, p2.

Next row (RS): K2, work 10 sts in seed st, w&t, work seed st to last 2 sts, p2.

Next row (RS): K2, work 5 sts in seed st, w&t, work seed st to last 2 sts, p2.

Next row (RS): K2, work seed st across (remove markers) to within 2 sts of end of row, k2.

Raised front shaping is now complete.

Continue working in St st on the 2 sts at beg and end of every row, with all others in seed st until piece from beginning measures (from side edge) 17½ in / 44.5 cm. End having completed a WS row.

Set-up for center front neck:

Next row (RS): K2, work 53 sts in seed st, k2tog, k3, work 53 sts in seed st, k2. [114 sts remain]

Next row (WS): P2, work 53 sts in seed st, p4, work 53 sts in seed st, p2.

Divide for front neck:

Next row (RS): K2, work 53 sts in seed st, k2. Place 57 sts for right front neck on a holder or waste yarn.

Left Front Neck Shaping

Row 1 (WS, decrease row): P2, p2tog, work in seed st to last 2 sts, p2.

Row 2 (RS): K2, work in seed st to last 3 sts, k3.

Row 3 (WS): P3, work in seed st to last 2 sts, p2.

Row 4 (RS, decrease row): K2, work in seed st to last 4 sts, k2tog, k2.

Row 5 (WS): P3, work in seed st to last 2 sts, p2.

Row 6 (RS): K2, work in seed st across to last 3 sts, k3.

Repeat rows 1–6, working decrease row every 3rd row 20 times total until 37 sts remain. Continue with no further decreases (if necessary) until piece from side seam measures 25 in / 63.5 cm or same as back to shoulder shaping. End having completed a RS row.

Left Shoulder Shaping

Next row (WS): P3, work in seed st across to last 10 sts, w&t, work seed st back to last 3 sts, k3.

Next row (WS): P3, work in seed st to within 20 sts of end, w&t, work seed st back to last 3 sts, k3.

Next row (WS): P3, work in seed st to within 30 sts of end, w&t, work seed st back to last 3 sts, k3.

Next row: Purl.

Next row: Knit.

Place sts on a holder or waste yarn.

Right Front Neck Shaping

Join yarn at (RS): K2, work 53 sts in seed st, k2.

Row 1 (WS, decrease row): P2, work in seed st to last 4 sts, p2togtbl (through the back loop), p2.

Row 2 (RS): K3, work in seed st to last 2 sts, k2.

Row 3 (WS): P2, work in seed st to last 3 sts, p3.

Row 4 (RS, decrease row): K2, ssk, work in seed st to last 2 sts, k2.

Row 5 (WS): P2, work in seed st to last 3 sts, p3.

Row 6 (RS): K3, work in seed st to last 2 sts, k2.

Continue working rows 1–6 as established, working a decrease every 3rd row 20 times total until 37 sts remain. Continue with no further decreases (if necessary) until piece from side seam measures same as other side. End having completed a WS row.

Right Shoulder Shaping

Next row (RS): K3, work seed st to within 10 sts of end, w&t, work seed st back to last 3 sts, p3.

Next row (RS): K3, work seed st to within 20 sts of end, w&t, work seed st back to last 3 sts, p3.

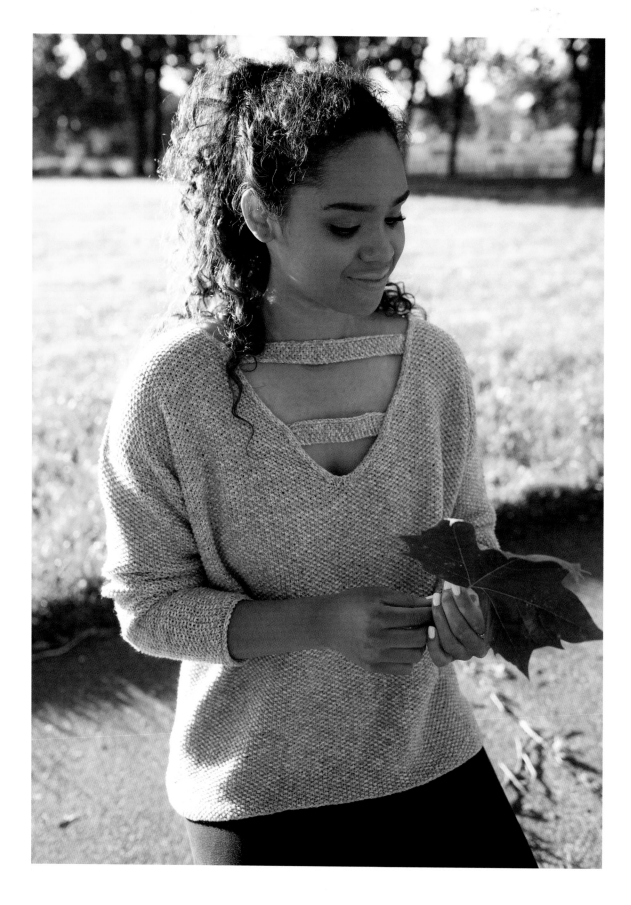

Next row (RS): K3, work seed st to within 30 sts of end, w&t, work seed st back to last 3 sts, p3.

Next row (RS): Knit.

Next row (WS): Purl.

Work the three-needle bind-off on shoulders from the RS for a decorative seam as shown in photo, or from the WS for a smoother look.

SLEEVES

Measure down 7 in / 18 cm from either side of shoulder and place a hanging marker on front and back. Join yarn on RS and pick up and knit 71 sts between markers. (Try [pick up 2, skip 1, pick up 1, skip 1]).

Next row (WS): Purl. (Counts as row 1.)

To work a decrease row on RS: K2, seed2tog, work seed st to last 4 sts, seed2tog, k2.

To work a decrease row on WS: P2, seed2tog, work seed st to last 4 sts, seed2tog, p2.

Work a decrease row every 9th row 17 times total to 37 sts. Sleeve should measure approx. 18 in / 45.5 cm. End having completed a WS row.

Next row (RS): Knit.

Next row (WS): Purl.

Bind off in knit on the RS.

Make other sleeve to match.

FRONT STRAPS

Note: Although approx. lengths are stated, straps can be any length to fit across front neck at any place of your choosing.

Cast on 7 sts, leaving an 8 in / 20.5 cm tail for stitching to front.

Row 1 (WS): P1, [k1, p1] 3 times.

Row 2 (RS): K2, p1, k1, p1, k2.

Repeat rows 1 and 2 until strip measures 4½ in / 11.5 cm. Leave an 8 in / 20.5 cm tail.

Make another strap to measure 8½ in / 21.5 cm.

FINISHING

Stitch side and underarm seams, using a mattress stitch from the RS.

Stitch straps on WS, under first 2 sts of front edge, first strap approx 1½ in / 4 cm above center front and the other approx 4½ in / 11.5 cm above center front.

Weave in ends. Steam lightly, or block according to directions on ball band.

Simple Shift with Two Belts

Sleek and shapely easy–knit shift. Wear it plain or add a belt.

SIZES

Juniors 3 (5, 7, 9) (11, 13, 15)

Instructions are written for size 3; all other sizes are in parentheses.

FINISHED MEASUREMENTS

Chest: 29 (32, 34, 35) (35½, 36, 38) in / 73.5 (81.5, 86.5, 89) (90, 91.5, 96.5) cm

Waist: 24 (24½ 25, 27) (28½, 30, 32) in / 61 (62, 63.5, 68.5) (72.5, 76, 81.5) cm

Hips: 28 (32, 33, 35) (36½, 38, 39) in / 71 (81.5, 84, 89) (92.5, 96.5, 99) cm

Back to waist length: 13½ (14½, 15, 15½) (15½, 16, 16) in / 34.5 (37, 38, 39.5) (39.5, 40.5, 40.5) cm

Total length: 30½ (32½, 33, 34) (34½, 35, 35½) in / 77.5 (82.5, 84, 86.5) (87.5, 89, 90) cm

YARN

Cascade Heritage Yarn; 3.5 oz / 100 g each approx. 437 yd / 400 m; 75% superwash merino, 25% nylon
- 3 skeins (all sizes) #5634 Mossy Rock

MATERIALS

- Size US 3 / 3.25 mm 24 in / 60 cm circular needle (*or size to obtain gauge*)
- Size US 3 / 3.25 mm 16 in / 40 cm circular needle
- Tapestry needle
- Waste yarn
- Pin-type markers
- Ring-type markers

GAUGE

30 sts and 38 rows to 4 in / 10 cm in St st

STITCH GUIDE

Three-needle bind-off. Turn pieces inside out and place live stitches on 2 parallel needles. Then knit 2 stitches together, one from each of the parallel needles. Knit another 2 stitches together, one from each needle. You now have 2 stitches on your right needle; use your left needle to pull the first stitch over the second and off the needle (one stitch bound off). Continue binding off in this manner (k2tog, bind off 1).

W&t. Wrap and turn; slip the next stitch, bring the yarn to the front (or back if a purl row), then put the stitch back on the left needle, turn and work back across next row. This will leave some stitches unworked.

PATTERN NOTES

- Pattern worked in the round from the bottom up.
- Front and back divided and worked separately from armhole.
- Sleeves and neckband worked in the round.

STITCH PATTERN

Twisted Rib

Row/rnd 1: [K1b, p1b] repeat across/around.

Repeat row/rnd 1, keeping knits over knits and purls over purls.

SHIFT

Cast on 270 (288, 300, 312) (324, 340, 348) sts.

Place a marker and join into a round, being careful not to twist sts.

Work [k1b, p1b] around until ribbing measures 1½–2 in / 4–5 cm (or desired length).

Next rnd (decrease rnd, all sizes): [K4, k2tog] to 225 (240, 250, 260) (270, 284, 290) sts.

Change to stockinette stitch.

Knit 112 (120, 125, 130) (135, 142, 145) sts, place different-color marker for side edge, continue to beginning of round (now other side edge *and* beginning of round).

Knit until piece measures 6 in / 15 cm from beginning, slipping markers as you come to them.

End at beg-of-rnd marker.

To work a decrease rnd: K1, ssk, knit to within 3 sts of side marker, k2tog, k1, slip marker, k1, ssk, knit to

within 3 sts of beginning of round, k2tog, k1. [4 sts decreased]

Work a decrease round now, then every 8th (7th, 6th, 8th) (8th, 8th, 10th) round 12 (14, 17, 14) (14, 14, 12) times *more* to 173 (180, 188, 200) (214, 224, 238) sts. Continue with no further decreases until length of skirt measures 17 (17½, 18, 18½) (19, 19, 19½) in / 43 (44.5, 45.5, 47) (48.5, 48.5, 49.5) cm from beginning (or desired length to waist).

Waist to Bust Shaping

To work an increase rnd: K1, M1, knit to within one stitch of side marker, M1, k1, slip marker, k1, M1, work around to within 1 st of beginning marker, M1, k1.

Work an increase round now, and every 6th (5th, 5th, 6th) (6th, 6th, 6th) round 10 (14, 16, 14) (14, 14, 12) times *more* to 217 (240, 256, 262) (274, 286, 290) sts. (On size 3 only, increase one more st at next marker to 218 sts.)

Continue with no further increases (if necessary) until bodice from waist measures 7½ (8½, 9, 9½) (9½, 9½, 9½) in / 19 (21.5, 23, 24) (24, 24, 24) cm (or desired length to underarm).

Divide for armholes:
Bind off 6 sts, then knit to side marker.

Remove marker and place next 109 (120, 128, 131) (137, 143, 146) sts on a holder or waste yarn. Front and back will now be worked separately in St st rows.

Armhole Shaping

Next row (WS): Bind off 6 sts, purl across. (For ease in measuring, hang a pin-type marker somewhere along the middle of the row.)

Next row (RS): K1, ssk, knit to last 3 sts, k2tog, k1.
Next row: Purl.

Repeat last 2 rows 2 (2, 3, 2) (2, 3, 2) times more to 91 (102, 108, 113) (119, 123, 128) sts.

Continue with no further decreases until piece from armhole measures 3 (3, 3, 3½) (3½, 3½, 3½) in / 7.5 (7.5, 7.5, 9) (9, 9, 9) cm. End having completed a WS row.

Neck Shaping

(RS): Knit across 68 (77, 81, 85) (90, 93, 97) sts. Place last 45 (52, 54, 57) (61, 63, 66) sts *just worked* on a holder or waste yarn for front neck and continue across row.

Working on right front sts only, work as follows:

Row 1 (WS): Purl across to last 3 sts, p2tog, p1.
Row 2 (RS): Knit.

Repeat rows 1 and 2 four times more. [5 sts decreased total]

Continue with no further decreases on 18 (20, 22, 23) (24, 25, 26) sts until piece from center neck measures 2½ in / 6.5 cm. End having completed a WS row.

Next row (WS): Purl to last 4 (4, 4, 4) (5, 5, 5) sts, w&t, knit back on RS.

Next row (WS): Purl to last 8 (8, 8, 8) (10, 10, 10) sts, w&t, knit back on RS.

Next row (WS): Purl to last 12 (12, 12, 12) (15, 15, 15) sts, w&t, knit back on RS.

Next row (WS): Purl to last 16 (16, 16, 16) (20, 20, 20) sts, w&t, knit back on RS.

Work across all sts, picking up wraps as you come to them.

Place sts on holder or waste yarn.

BACK

Place back sts on needle and join new yarn at RS.

Bind off 6 sts at the beginning of the next 2 rows.
   (Hang a pin-type marker somewhere along the first bind-off row for ease in measuring.)

Next row (RS): K1, ssk, knit to last 3 sts, k2tog, k1.

Next row: Purl.

Repeat last 2 rows 2 (2, 3, 2) (2, 3, 2) times more to 91 (102, 108, 113) (119, 123, 128) sts.

Shoulder Shaping

(RS): Knit to last 4 (4, 4, 4) (5, 5, 5) sts, w&t, purl back on WS.

Next row (RS): Knit to last 8 (8, 8, 8) (10, 10, 10) sts, w&t, purl back on WS.

Next row (RS): Knit to last 12 (12, 12, 12) (15, 15, 15) sts, w&t, purl back on WS.

Next row (RS): Knit to last 16 (16, 16, 16) (20, 20, 20) sts, w&t, purl back on WS.

Work across all sts, picking up wraps as you come to them (place needle under wrap first and knit it together with st on needle).

Place all sts on holder or waste yarn.

Join new yarn to WS at neck edge and work other shoulder as follows:

Row 1 (WS): P1, p2tog, purl across.

Next row (RS): Knit.

Repeat rows 1 and 2 four times more. [5 sts decreased total]

Continue with no further decreases on 18 (20, 22, 23) (24, 25, 26) sts until piece from center neck measures 2½ in / 6.5 cm.

End having completed a RS row.

Continue with no further decreases until piece from armhole measures 4½ (4½, 4½, 5) (5, 5, 5) in / 11.5 (11.5, 11.5, 13) (13, 13, 13) cm. End having completed a WS row.

Neck Shaping

(RS): Work across 68 (77, 81, 85) (90, 93, 97) sts. Place last 45 (52, 54, 57) (61, 63, 66) sts *just worked* on a holder or waste yarn for front neck and continue across row.

Working on right front sts only, work as follows:

Row 1 (WS): Purl to last 3 sts, p2tog, p1.
Row 2 (RS): Knit.
Repeat rows 1 and 2 four times more. [5 sts decreased total]

Continue with no further decreases on 18 (20, 22, 23) (24, 25, 26) sts until piece from center neck measures 1 in / 2.5 cm. End having completed a WS row.

Shoulder Shaping

(RS): Knit to last 4 (4, 4, 4) (5, 5, 5) sts, w&t, purl back on WS.
Next row (RS): Knit to last 8 (8, 8, 8) (10, 10, 10) sts, w&t, purl back on WS.
Next row (RS): Knit to last 12 (12, 12, 12) (15, 15, 15) sts, w&t, purl back on WS.
Next row (RS): Knit to last 16 (16, 16, 16) (20, 20, 20) sts, w&t, purl back on WS.
Work across all sts, picking up wraps as you come to them.

Place all sts on holder or waste yarn.

Join new yarn to WS at neck edge and work other shoulder as follows:
Row 1 (WS): P1, p2tog, purl across.
Next row (RS): Knit.
Repeat rows 1 and 2 four times more. [5 sts decreased total]
Continue with no further decreases on 18 (20, 22, 23) (24, 25, 26) sts until piece from center neck measures 1½ in / 4 cm. End having completed a RS row.

Next row (WS): Purl to last 4 (4, 4, 4) (5, 5, 5) sts, w&t, knit back on RS.
Next row (WS): Purl to last 8 (8, 8, 8) (10, 10, 10) sts, w&t, knit back on RS.
Next row (WS): Purl to last 12 (12, 12, 12) (15, 15, 15) sts, w&t, knit back on RS.
Next row (WS): Purl to last 16 (16, 16, 16) (20, 20, 20) st, w&t, knit back on RS.
Work across all sts, picking up wraps as you come to them.

Join Front and Back
Use the three-needle bind-off to connect the shoulder sts together.

NECK BORDER
With 16 in / 40 cm circular needle, slip back neck sts from waste yarn to needle. Join yarn and pick up and knit stitch for stitch to front neck sts, knit across 45 (52, 54, 57) (61, 63, 66) front neck sts, pick up and knit st for st to back neck, knit across 45 (52, 54, 57) (61, 63, 66) sts, place marker. Adjust, if necessary to an even number of sts.
Work [k1b, p1b] rib for 1½ in / 4 cm (or desired length of neck border). Bind off loosely in rib.

ARMBAND
With 16 in / 40 cm circular needle, beginning at underarm, pick up and knit stitch for stitch around armhole. Adjust, if necessary, to an even number of sts.

Work in [k1b, p1b] rib until armband measures ½ in / 1.25 cm (or desired length). Bind off loosely in [k1, p1] rib.
Make second to match.

FINISHING
Weave in ends and steam lightly, or block according to directions on ball band.

Reversible Cabled Brioche Belt with Button Closure

SIZES

Junior 3 (5, 7, 9) (11, 13, 15)

Instructions are written for size 3; all other sizes are in parentheses.

FINISHED MEASUREMENTS

3 in / 7.5 cm x 23 (23½ 24, 26) (27½, 29, 31) in / 58.5 (59.5, 61, 66) (70, 73.5, 78.5) cm

YARN

Cascade Heritage Yarn; 3.5 oz / 100 g each approx. 437 yd / 400 m; 75% superwash merino, 25% nylon
- 1 skein #5634 Mossy Rock

MATERIALS

- Size US 3 / 3.25 mm needles (*or size to obtain gauge*)
- Cable needle
- Tapestry needle
- Row counter
- 5 small buttons

GAUGE

30 sts and 38 rows to 4 in / 10 cm in St st (gauge not critical for this project)

STITCH GUIDE

BrC6F. Brioche Cable; slip 6 sts (include yo's as stitches) onto CN and hold at front, [slip 1, yo, k2tog] 2 times, slip sts from CN back to left needle and [slip 1, yo, k2tog] 2 times.

W&t. Wrap and turn; slip the next stitch, bring the yarn to the front (or back if a purl row), then put the stitch back on the left needle, turn and work back across next row. This will leave some stitches unworked.

STITCH PATTERN

Twisted Rib

Row/rnd 1: [K1b, p1b] repeat across/around.

Repeat row/rnd 1, keeping knits over knits and purls over purls.

PATTERN NOTES

- As this is a reversible pattern and a challenge to "read" the work, a row counter is an invaluable tool to keep track of rows.

BELT

Note: Reversible Brioche Cable pattern is a multiple of 12 + 2.

Cast on 26 sts.

Set-up row: K1, [slip 1, yo, k1] repeat to last st, k1.

Rows 1–10: K1, [slip 1, yo, k2tog] repeat to last st, k1. [38 sts]

Row 11: K1, BrC6F, [slip 1, yo, k2tog] 4 times, BrC6F, k1.

Rows 12–22: K1, [slip 1, yo, k2tog] repeat to last st, k1.

Row 23: K1, [slip 1, yo, k2tog] 4 times, Brc6F, [slip 1, yo, k2tog] 4 times, k1.

Work rows 1–23 until length of belt is 23 (23½, 24, 26) (27½, 29, 31) in / 58.5 (59.5, 61, 66) (70, 73.5, 78.5) cm (or 1–2 in / 2.5–5 cm less than actual waist). End on row 17, if possible. Belt will be stretchy but is meant to be decorative, so a little loose is okay. Bind off in pattern, omitting yo's.

Buttonholes

Pick up and knit 27 sts across one end of belt.

Next row (make buttonholes): K1, [yo, k2tog, k4] 4 times, yo, k2tog.

Knit one row and then bind off.

Pick up 27 sts at other end. Knit 3 rows, then bind off.

FINISHING

Sew buttons opposite buttonholes; weave in ends. No blocking necessary, but steam lightly if desired.

Twisted Rib Tie Belt

SIZES

One size fits all Juniors

FINISHED MEASUREMENTS

3 in / 7.5 cm wide x 56–58 in / 142-147.5 cm long

YARN

Cascade Heritage Yarn; 3.5 oz / 100 g each approx. 437 yd /400 m; 75% superwash merino, 25% nylon
- 1 skein #5634 Mossy Rock

MATERIALS

- Size US 3 / 3.25 mm needles (*or size to obtain gauge*)
- Tapestry needle

GAUGE

30 sts and 38 rows to 4 in / 10 cm in St st (gauge not critical for this project)

BELT

Note: Slip the first st of every row as if to purl with yarn in front, then put yarn in back before knitting next st. The last st of every row will be knit in the regular way without a twist.

Cast on 30 sts.

Row 1: Slip 1, [k1, p1] repeat to last st, k1.

Next row: Slip 1, [k1b, p1b] repeat to last st, k1.

Repeat last row for pattern.

When belt measures 52–58 in / 132–147.5 (or desired length, long enough to tie), bind off.

FINISHING

Weave in any ends and steam lightly, or block according to directions on ball band.

Summer Dress

Find flirty comfort in a stylish dress for school or play. The full skater skirt and detailed spaghetti-strap top make this a must-have for every teenager's wardrobe. Top and skirt can be knit separately.

SIZES
Juniors 3 (5, 7, 9) (11, 13, 15)
Instructions are written for size 3; all other sizes are in parentheses.

FINISHED MEASUREMENTS
Chest: 29 (32, 34, 35) (35½, 36, 38) in / 73.5 (81.5, 86.5, 89) (90, 91.5, 96.5) cm
Waist: 24 (24½, 25, 27) (28½, 30, 32) in / 61 (62, 63.5, 68) (72.5, 76, 81.5) cm
Back to waist length: 13½ (14½, 15, 15½) (15½, 16, 16) in / 34.5 (37, 38, 39.5) (39.5, 40.5, 40.5) cm
Total length: 30½ (32½, 33, 34) (34½, 35, 35½) in / 77.5 (82.5, 84, 86.5) (87.5, 89, 90) cm

YARN
Heritage Silk # 5732, Delphinium Blue; 3.5 oz / 100 g each approx. 437 yds / 400 meters; 85% superwash merino wool / 15% silk
- 4 (4, 4, 5) (5, 5, 5) skeins

MATERIALS
- Size US 3 / 3.25 mm 40 in / 101.5 circular needle (*or size to obtain gauge*)
- Size US 3 / 3.25 mm 24 in / 60 cm circular needles
- Tapestry needle
- Waste yarn
- Pin-type markers
- Two different color ring-type markers
- Size G or H / 4 or 5 mm crochet hook for provisional cast-on chain (no other crochet skills needed)

GAUGE
26 sts and 36 rows to 4 in / 10 cm in St st

STITCH GUIDE

Provisional cast-on. With waste yarn and crochet hook, chain desired number of stitches plus a few more and finish off. Pick up and knit stitches through the back loop of the chain. For those who don't want to crochet, cast on desired number of stitches and knit a few rows in waste yarn before continuing in project yarn.

Knitted cast-on. Start with a slipknot (or live stitch) on the left-hand needle. Work a knit stitch with the right-hand needle, but do not slip it off the left needle. Instead, place the loop from the right needle back onto the left needle (one stitch cast on). Continue until the desired number of stitches are on the left needle.

PATTERN NOTES

- Skirt is worked in the round from the waist down, with provisional cast-on.
- Top is picked up and worked in the round to armholes, then front and back are worked separately.
- Neck and armholes finished with attached I-cord.

SKIRT

Begin at waist with 24 in / 60 cm needle and provisionally cast on 156 (160, 164, 176) (186, 196, 208) sts. Place a marker and join into a round being careful not to twist sts.

Knit 6 rnds.

For all sizes, every 7th rnd will increase by 32 sts.

Rnd 7: Work increase rnd as follows for your size:

Size 3: K7, [k4, M1], k7, [k4, M1] 30 times, k7, [k4, M1], k7.

Size 5: [K5, M1] 32 times.

Size 7: K2, [k5, M1] 32 times, k2.

Size 9: K4, [k5, M1], k4, [k5, M1] 30 times, k4, [k5, M1], k4.

Size 11: K6, [k5, M1], k7, [k5, M1] 30 times, k7, [k5, M1], k6.

Size 13: K2, [k6, M1] 32 times, k2.

Size 15: K4, [k6, M1], k4, [k6, M1] 30 times, k4, [k6, M1], k4.

Knit 6 rounds.

Increase next rnd as before, *except* add one stitch before each M1 as follows:

Size 3: K7, [k5, M1], k7, [k5, M1] 30 times, k7, [k5, M1], k7.

Size 5: [K6, M1] 32 times.

Size 7: K2, [k6, M1] 32 times, k2.

Size 9: K4, [k6, M1], k4, [k6, M1] 30 times, k4, [k6, M1], k4.

Size 11: K6, [k6, M1], k7, [k6, M1] 30 times, k7, [k6, M1], k6.

Size 13: K2, [k7, M1] 32 times, k2.

Size 15: K4, [k7, M1], k4, [k7, M1] 30 times, k4, [k6, M1], k4.

Knit 6 rounds.

Increase next rnd as before, *except* add one stitch before each M1 as follows:

Size 3: K7, [k6, M1], k7, [k6, M1] 30 times, k7, [k6, M1], k7.

Size 5: [K7, M1] 32 times.

Size 7: K2, [k7, M1] 32 times, k2.

Size 9: K4, [k7, M1], k4, [k7, M1] 30 times, k4, [k7, M1], k4.

Size 11: K6, [k7, M1], k7, [k7, M1] 30 times, k7, [k7, M1], k6.

Size 13: K2, [k8, M1] 32 times, k2.

Size 15: K4, [k8, M1], k4, [k8, M1] 30 times, k4, [k7, M1], k4.

Work an increase rnd every 7th rnd as established (adding one stitch before each M1) until skirt measures approx. 16½ (17, 17, 18) (18½, 18½, 18½) in / 42 (43, 43, 45.5) (47, 47, 47) cm from cast-on (or desired length from waist). Use 40 in / 101.5 cm needle when sts become too crowded. The skirt will automatically circle no matter what length you desire.

Next rnd: Purl all sts.

Next 2 rnds: Knit all sts.

Repeat last 3 rnds once more, then purl 1 round and bind off loosely knitwise.

BODICE

With 24 in / 60 cm needle, unpick provisional cast-on and join new yarn at beg-of-rnd marker.

Next rnd: Purl all sts.

Next 2 rnds: Knit all sts.

Repeat last 3 rnds, then purl 1 round, decreasing 1 st (p2tog) at end of rnd. [155 (159, 163, 175) (185, 195, 207) sts remain]

Begin pattern (on an odd number of sts) for all sizes as follows:

Rnd 1: K1, [yo, sl 1, k1, yo, psso (pass the slipped st over the k1 and the yo)] repeat around.

Rnd 2: K1, drop yo from previous rnd , [k2 (if it's easier, go ahead and knit the second stitch through the back loop), drop yo], repeat to last 2 sts, k2.

Rnd 3: K2, [yo, sl 1, k1, yo, psso], repeat to last st, k1.

Rnd 4: [K2, drop yo], repeat to last 3 sts, k3.

Work rnds 1–4 until band measures 4½ (4½, 4½, 4½) (4½, 5, 5) in / 11.5 (11.5, 11.5, 11.5) (11.5, 13, 13) cm. End after completing a rnd 1 or 3.

Set-up pattern at center back and center front:

Work in pattern as established over first 23 (25, 29, 29) (31, 31, 33) sts, place marker, knit 16 (14, 12, 14) (15, 17, 19) sts, place different color marker for side, knit 16

(15, 12, 15) (16, 18, 19) sts, place marker, pattern over next 45 (51, 57, 59) (61, 63, 65) sts, place marker, knit 16 (15, 12, 15) (16, 18, 19) sts, place other side marker, knit 16 (14, 12, 14) (15, 17, 19) sts, place marker, work in pattern over last 23 (25, 29, 29) (31, 31, 33) sts. (**Note:** some numbers are not symmetrical to allow for an odd number of sts in each pattern section.)

Increases will occur before and after each side marker, and before and after patterned sections at center front and center back. 8 sts increase per rnd as follows:

Next rnd (increase rnd): Pattern to first marker, slip marker, M1, knit to within 1 st of side marker, M1, k1, slip marker, M1, knit to next marker, M1, slip marker, pattern to next marker, slip marker, M1, knit to within 1 st of side marker, M1, k1, slip marker, M1, knit to next marker, M1, slip marker, pattern to end.

Continue in rnds as established, working an increase rnd every 6th (6th, 5th, 6th) (6th, 8th, 8th) rnd 3 (5, 6, 5) (5, 4, 4) times more to 187 (207, 219, 223) (233, 235, 247) sts.

Continue (if necessary) with no further increases until piece from patterned belt-band measures 3 (4½, 4½, 4½) (4½, 4½, 4½) in / 7.5 (11.5, 11.5, 11.5) (11.5, 11.5, 11.5) cm (or desired length to armhole). End having completed a rnd 1 or 3 (very important) and at the end of rnd, at center back marker, cut yarn.

Divide for front and back:

Slip across remaining back sts to side marker, place all front sts on a spare needle or waste yarn.

Working in rows on back sts only, join new yarn on WS of back and bind off (in purl) 6 sts, keep pattern correct across middle section (see row directions below), then purl to end.

BACK

Next row (RS): Bind off 6, knit to pattern, pattern across center sts, knit to end.

Center pattern, row by row directions:

Row 1 (RS): K1, [yo, sl 1, k1, yo, psso (pass the slipped st over the knit 1 and the yo)] repeat across.

Row 2: [P2, drop yo] repeat to last st, p1.

Row 3: K2, [yo, sl 1, k1, yo, psso] repeat to last st, k1.

Row 4: P3, [drop yo, p2] repeat across.

Work center back pattern in rows, keeping pattern to left of center back marker as the beginning of the row directions, and sts to the right of center back marker as end of row directions.

Next row (WS): Purl across to pattern, work pattern across center back sts, purl to end.

Next row (RS): K1, ssk, knit across to pattern at center back, work pattern, knit to within 3 sts of end of row, k2tog, k1.

Repeat last 2 rows until all St sts have been decreased away and center 46 (50, 58, 58) (62, 62, 66) pattern sts remain. End having completed a WS row.

I-cord bind-off (RS): From first stitch, use the knitted cast-on to cast on 3 sts. *K3, ssk, slip 4 sts back to left needle. Repeat from * across. When 4 sts remain (after last k3, ssk), place sts on pin-type marker or waste yarn. Cut yarn.

FRONT

Place front sts on needle, join new yarn at underarm on WS.

Next row (WS): Bind off 6 sts, purl across to pattern, work pattern across center front sts, purl to end.

Next row (RS): Bind off 6 sts, knit to pattern, pattern across center sts, knit to end.

Next row (WS): Purl across to pattern, work pattern across center back sts, purl to end.

Next row (RS): K1, ssk, knit across to pattern at center back, work pattern, knit to within 3 sts of end of row, k2tog, k1.

Repeat last 2 rows until all St sts have been decreased away and center 45 (51, 57, 59) (61, 63, 65) pattern sts remain. End having completed a WS row.

I-cord bind-off (RS): From first stitch, use the knitted cast-on to cast on 3 sts. *K3, ssk, slip 4 sts back to left needle. Repeat from * across. When 4 sts remain (after last k3, ssk), place sts on pin-type marker or waste yarn. Cut yarn.

SLEEVE EDGING AND STRAPS

From RS at center of underarm, pick up and knit one st for every row to top or front, cast on 36 sts for strap (equals about 6 in / 15 cm of I-cord), continue picking up sts at other side and end at underarm.

From first picked up stitch, use the knitted cast-on to cast on 3 sts and work attached I-cord around: *k3, ssk, slip 4 sts back to left needle, repeat from * across.

Graft or stitch ends of I-cord at underarm.

Repeat for other side, making sure to cast on the same number of sts for other shoulder strap.

FINISHING

Weave in loose ends and steam lightly, or block according to directions on ball band.

Sunset and Lace

Adorned with an easy lace border, this scooped-neck, striped tank top is knit in the round from the bottom up with I-cord finish around neck and armholes.

SIZES
Juniors 3 (5, 7, 9) (11, 13, 15)
Instructions are written for size 3; all other sizes are in parentheses.

FINISHED MEASUREMENTS
Chest: 29 (32, 34, 35) (35½, 36, 38) in / 73.5 (81.5, 86.5, 89) (90, 91.5, 96.5) cm
Total length: 20 (20½, 21, 22) (22½, 23, 24) in / 51 (52, 53.5, 56) (57, 58.5, 61) cm

YARN
Cascade Heritage Silk; 3.5 oz / 100 g each approx. 437 yd / 400 m; 85% superwash merino, 15% mulberry silk
- 2 skeins #5682 White (A)
- 2 skeins #5716 Autumn Sunset (B)

MATERIALS
- Size US 3 / 3.25 mm 29 in / 73.5 cm circular needle (*or size to obtain gauge*)
- Two size US 3 / 3.25 mm double-pointed needles to work lace border (optional; you could also use a circular)
- Tapestry needle
- Waste yarn
- 6 or 7 pin-type markers
- 3 or more ring-type markers in 2 colors

GAUGE
28 sts and 38 rows to 4 in / 10 cm in St st

STITCH GUIDE
I-cord bind-off. At beg of rnd, cast on 3 sts. *Carry yarn around back and k2, ssk, slip 3 sts back to left needle, repeat from *. When 3 sts remain, graft to beginning of cord.

Sl2-k1-p2sso. Slip 2 sts, k1, then pass the 2 slipped sts over the knit st.

Three-needle bind-off. Turn pieces inside out and place live stitches on 2 parallel needles. Then knit 2 stitches together, one from each of the parallel needles. Knit another 2 stitches together, one from each needle. You now have 2 stitches on your right needle; use your left needle to pull the first stitch over the second and off the needle (one stitch bound off). Continue binding off in this manner (k2tog, bind off 1).

W&t. Wrap and turn; slip the next stitch, bring the yarn to the front (or back if a purl row), then put the stitch back on the left needle, turn and work back across row. Some stitches will be left unworked.

Wyif. Work with yarn held in front as if to purl.

STITCH PATTERN

Lace Pattern

Cast on 19 sts.

Row 1 (RS): Sl1 wyif, k2, [yo, k2tog] twice, k3, k2tog, yo, k1, yo, ssk, yo, k4. [20 sts]

Row 2 (WS): K4, p6, k5, [yo, k2tog] twice, k1.

Row 3: Sl1 wyif, k2, [yo, k2tog] twice, k2, k2tog, yo, k3, yo, ssk, yo, k2, [yo] twice, k2. [23 sts]

Row 4: K3, p1, k2, p8, k4, [yo, k2tog] twice, k1.

Row 5: Sl1 wyif, k2, [yo, k2tog] twice, k1, k2tog, yo, k5, yo, ssk, yo, k6. [24 sts]

Row 6: Bind off 2 sts, k3, p13, k3, [yo, k2tog] twice, k1. [22 sts]

Row 7: Sl1 wyif, k2, [yo, k2tog] twice, k2tog, yo, k7, yo, ssk, yo, k2, [yo] twice, k2. [25 sts]

Row 8: K3, p1, k2, p11, k3, [yo, k2tog] twice, k1.

Row 9: Sl1 wyif, k2, [yo, k2tog] twice, k1, yo, k9, yo, ssk, yo, k6. [27 sts]

Row 10: Bind off 2 sts, k3, p13, k3, [yo, k2tog] twice, k1. [25 sts]

Row 11: Sl1 wyif, k2, [yo, k2tog] twice, k1, yo, ssk, k2, sl2-k1-p2sso, k2, yo, ssk, yo, k2, [yo] twice, k2.

Row 12: K3, p1, k3, p9, k4, [yo, k2tog] twice, k1.

Row 13: Sl1 wyif, k2, [yo, k2tog] twice, k2, yo, ssk, sl2-k1-p2sso, [k2tog, yo] twice, k7. [23 sts]

Row 14: Bind off 4 sts, k3, p5, k5, [yo, k2tog] twice, k1. [19 sts]

Row 15: Sl1 wyif, k2, [yo, k2tog] twice, k3, yo, sl2-k1-p2sso, yo, k2tog, yo, k4.

Row 16: K4, p4, k6, [yo, k2tog] twice, k1.

Repeat rows 1–16 for pattern.

PATTERN NOTES

- Lace border worked separately, then joined with work in progress.
- Worked in the round from the bottom up.
- Front and back divided and worked separately from armhole.
- Sleeve and neckbands worked in the round with I-cord bind-off.

TOP

Notes:

- Do not cut yarn between rounds, but carry loosely up center back, twisting every (or every other) round.
- To avoid a color jog at the center back, at the end of first round of a color change, slip marker, then pick up the back leg of the st from the round below, place on needle and knit it tog with first st of round.
- Color Sequence: Knit 4 rounds with A, knit 4 rounds with B. Repeat.

With B, cast on 288 (304, 320, 336) (336, 336, 355) sts. Place a marker for center back and join into a round, being careful not to twist sts. Knit in rounds until piece from beginning measures 4½–5 in / 11.5–13

cm. You can steam out the rolled edge at this point for ease in measuring. Do not cut yarn, but set aside to make lace.

Lace

With A and double-pointed needles or 16 in / 40 cm circular, work Lace Pattern rows 1–16, 18 (19, 20, 21) (21, 21 22) times, until top edge has 288 (304, 320, 336) (336, 336, 352) "chain" sts. (Helpful hint: Hang a pin-type marker every 50 chain sts for ease in counting.) Bind off in knit on RS.

Place lace over knitting at beg of round marker, and insert needle into top of lace "chain stitch" first, then into st on needle and knit the 2 together. Pick up and knit st for st around in this manner, until beg of round marker (lace is now joined and will ruffle slightly). On next round, place a different color marker for side shaping as follows:

Knit 72 (76, 80, 84) (84, 84, 88) sts, place side marker, knit 144 (152, 160, 168) (168, 168, 176) sts for front, place other side marker, finish round to center back.

Work 2 more rounds in B.

To work a decrease round: *Work to within 3 sts of side marker, ssk, k1, slip marker, k1, k2tog, repeat from * once more, finish round to center back.

Change colors every 4 rounds and, *at the same time*, work a decrease round every 4th (4th, 5th, 4th) (5th, 5th, 6th) round 21 (21, 21, 23) (22, 21, 21) times until 204 (216, 236, 244) (248, 252, 268) sts remain. Continue on these sts (if necessary) until piece from beginning measures 14 (14½, 15, 15½) (16, 16½, 17½) in / 35.5 (37, 38, 39.5) (40.5, 42, 44.5) cm (*or desired length to armhole*). End after working 2 rounds of color. Only Color B is used for the first 4½–5 inches, then 4-row stripes begin for the rest of the piece.

Divide for front and back:

Keeping stripe pattern correct, knit across to within 7 sts of side marker, bind off 14 sts (remove marker), continue around front to within 7 sts of other side marker, bind off 14, knit to center back. Remove marker and knit across to armhole edge. (This side will have one extra color row, it's okay.) Place all front sts on a holder or waste yarn. The front and back will now be worked separately in St st rows.

BACK

Armhole Shaping

Next row (WS): Purl.

Next row (RS): K1, ssk, knit to last 3 sts, k2tog, k1.

Work last 2 rows 3 times more to 80 (86, 96, 100) (102, 104, 112) sts.

Continue on these sts until work from bind-off measures 4½ (4½, 4½, 5) (5, 5, 5) in / 11.5 (11.5, 11.5, 13) (13, 13, 13) cm, end having completed a WS row.

Back Neck Shaping

(RS): Knit 28 (30, 32, 34) (35, 35, 38), bind off center 24 (26, 32, 32) (32, 34, 36) sts, knit to end.

Next row (WS): Purl to last 3 sts, p2tog, p1.

Next row (RS): K1, ssk, knit to end.

Repeat last 2 rows, decreasing 1 st at neck edge every row until 14 (14, 14, 16) (17, 18, 20) shoulder sts remain. Continue on these sts (if necessary) until armhole measures 6½ (6½, 6½, 7) (7, 7, 7) in / 16.5

(16.5, 16.5, 18) (18, 18, 18) cm. Place sts on a holder or waste yarn.

Join appropriate color yarn on WS at neck edge.

(WS): P1, p2togtbl (through back loop), purl across.

Next row (RS): Knit to last 3 sts, k2tog, k1.

Repeat last 2 rows, decreasing 1 st at neck edge every row until 14 (14, 14, 16) (17, 18, 20) shoulder sts remain. Continue on these sts (if necessary) until armhole measures 6½ (6½, 6½, 7) (7, 7, 7) in / 16.5 (16.5, 16.5, 18) (18, 18, 18) cm. Place sts on a holder or waste yarn.

FRONT

Place sts from holder on needle and join appropriate color yarn on WS.

Armhole Shaping

Next row (RS): K1, ssk, knit to last 3 sts, k2tog, k1.

Next row (WS): Purl.

Work last 2 rows 3 times more to 80 (86, 96, 100) (102, 104, 112) sts.

Continue on these sts until work from bind-off measures 2½ (2½, 2½, 3) (3, 3, 3) in / 5 (5, 5, 7.5) (7.5, 7.5, 7.5) cm (or 4 in / 10 cm less than back at shoulder). End having completed a WS row.

Front Neck Shaping
(RS): Knit 28 (30, 32, 34) (35, 35, 38) sts, bind off center 24 (26, 32, 32) (32, 34, 36) sts, knit across.
Next row (WS): Purl.
Next row (RS): K1, ssk, knit to end.
Repeat last 2 rows, decreasing 1 st at neck edge *every other row* until 14 (14, 14, 16) (17, 18, 20) shoulder sts remain. Continue on these sts (if necessary) until armhole measures 6½ (6½, 6½, 7) (7, 7, 7) in / 16.5 (16.5, 16.5, 18) (18, 18, 18) cm. Place sts on a holder or waste yarn.

Join appropriate color yarn on WS at neck edge.
(WS): Purl.
Next row (RS): Knit to last 3 sts, k2tog, k1.

Repeat last 2 rows, decreasing 1 st at neck edge *every other row* until 14 (14, 14, 16) (17, 18, 20) shoulder sts remain. Continue on these sts (if necessary) until armhole measures 6½ (6½, 6½, 7) (7, 7, 7) in / 16.5 (16.5, 16.5, 18) (18, 18, 18) cm.
Use the three-needle bind-off to connect shoulder stitches.

ARMHOLE BORDERS
With circular needle and color of choice, begin at underarm and pick up and knit st for st around (no need to mark beg of round). From first picked up st, cast on 3 sts, then begin I-cord bind-off as follows: *K2, ssk, slip 3 sts back to left needle, bring yarn around back and repeat from * until 3 sts remain. Graft to beg of cord. Repeat for second armhole.

NECK BORDER
Begin at center back (or location of choice) and work same as armhole borders.

FINISHING
Weave in any ends and steam lightly, or block according to directions on ball band.

Top-Down Raglan Sweater

This oversized cowl-neck sweater with cables has lots of room, just the way you like it. Make it long, for warmth on winter days, or short and cropped to top off your favorite jeans.

SIZES

Small (Medium, Large)
Sized to fit Juniors 3–5 (7–9) (11–15)
Instructions are written for size Small; all other sizes are in parentheses.

FINISHED MEASUREMENTS

Chest: 38 (40, 42) in / 96.5 (101.5, 106.5) cm
Cropped length: 17½ (18½, 19½) in / 44.5 (47, 49.5) cm

YARN

Cascade 220 Superwash; 3.5 oz / 100 g each approx. 220 yd / 200 m; 100% superwash wool
- 8 skeins #881 Then There's Mauve

MATERIALS

- Size US 6 / 4 mm 24 in / 60 cm circular needle (*or size to obtain gauge*)
- Size US 6 / 4 mm 16 in / 40 cm circular needle
- Size US 4 / 3.5 mm set of double-pointed needles (or any needle for knitting cuffs in the round)
- Size US 4 / 3.5 mm 24 in / 60 cm circular needle
- Tapestry needle
- Waste yarn
- Pin-type markers
- 8 ring-type markers

GAUGE

22 sts and 28 rows to 4 in / 10 cm on size US 6 / 4 mm in Double Moss stitch

STITCH GUIDE

C12B. Slip next 6 sts onto CN and hold at back, k6, then knit 6 from CN.

STITCH PATTERNS

Twisted 2x2 Rib
[K2b, p2b] repeat around on every round.

Garter Ridges [over 6 (7, 8) sts]
Rnds 1 and 2: K1, p4 (5, 6), k1.
Rnds 3 and 4: K6 (7, 8).

Double Moss (over 6 sts)
Rnd 1: [K1, p1] 3 times.
Rnd 2: [K1, p1] 3 times.
Rnd 3: [P1, k1] 3 times.
Rnd 4: [P1, k1] 3 times.
Repeat rnds 1–4.

Cable (over 16 sts)
Rnds 1–15: P2, k12, p2.
Rnd 16: P2, C12B, p2.
Repeat rnds 1–16 for pattern.

PATTERN NOTES

- Worked in the round from the top down.
- Sleeves picked up and worked in the round to cuff.
- Raglan increases are made on either side of decorative k1. Use markers to keep your place.

SWEATER

Begin at neck: With 16 in / 40 cm needle, cast on 212 (220, 232) sts. Place a marker and join into a round, being careful not to twist sts.
Set-up rnd: [K2, p2] around.
All other rnds: [K2b, p2b] around.
Work in twisted 2x2 rib until collar measures 9½ (10, 10½) in / 24 (25.5, 26.5) cm (or desired length).
Keep beg-of-round marker throughout.

Next round, decrease rnd, directions for your size as follows:
Small: K1, [k2tog 4 times, k1] 23 times, k2tog, k2. (120 sts)
Medium: K2, [k2tog 4 times, k1] 24 times, k2. (124 sts)
Large: [K2tog 4 times, k1] 24 times, [k2tog] 8 times. (128 sts)

Note: Work double moss st on either side of markers until enough sts have been increased, then change to next pattern in sequence. Round by round directions have been written out for you to get started.
Rnd 1: K1, place marker, *p1, k1, p4 (5, 6), k1, [k1, p1] 3 times, p2, k12, p2, [k1, p1] 3 times, k1, p4 (5, 6), k1, p1, place marker, k1, place marker, p2, k12, p2**, place marker, k1, place marker, work from * to **. (8 markers separate out the knit stitches that will remain constant throughout the raglan increases and divide the front, back, and sleeves.)
Rnd 2, increase rnd: *Slip marker, k1, slip marker, M1, p1, k1, p4 (5, 6), k1, [k1, p1] 3 times, p2, k12, p2, [k1, p1] 3 times, k1, p4 (5, 6), k1, p1, M1, slip marker, k1, slip marker, M1, p2, k12, p2, M1, work from * to end.
Rnd 3: *Slip marker, k1, slip marker, k1, p1, k6 (7, 8), [p1, k1] 3 times, p2, k12, p2, [p1, k1] 3 times, k6 (7, 8), p1, k1, slip marker, k1, slip marker, k1, p2, k12, p2, k1, slip marker, k1, work from * to end.
Rnd 4, increase rnd: *Slip marker, k1, slip marker, M1, p1, k6 (7, 8), [p1, k1] 3 times, p2, k12, p2, [p1, k1] 3

times, k6 (7, 8), p1, M1, slip marker, k1, slip marker, M1, p2, k12, p2, M1, work from * to end.

Rnd 5: *Slip marker, k1, slip marker, k1, p1, k1, k1, p4 (5, 6), k1, [k1, p1] 3 times, p2, k12, p2, [k1, p1] 3 times, k1, p4 (5, 6), k1, k1, p1, k1, slip marker, k1, slip marker, k1, p1, p2, k12, p2, p1, k1, work from * to end.

Rnd 6, increase rnd: *Slip marker, k1, slip marker, M1, p1, k1, p1, k1, p4 (5, 6), k1, [k1, p1] 3 times, p2, k12, p2, [k1, p1] 3 times, k1, p4 (5, 6), k1, p1, k1, p1, M1, slip marker, k1, slip marker, M1, p1, k1, p2, k12, p2, k1, p1, M1, work from * to end.

Rnd 7: *Slip marker, k1, slip marker, [k1, p1] twice, k6 (7, 8), [p1, k1] 3 times, p2, k12, p2, [p1, k1] 3 times, k6 (7, 8), [p1, k1] twice, slip marker, k1, slip marker, k1, p1, k1, p2, k12, p2, k1, p1, k1, work from * to end.

Continue as established, increasing 8 sts per round every other round and *at the same time* work patterns as established into added sts.

Note: Front and back pattern sequence will begin between brackets and finish as follows: Moss, Garter, Moss, Cable, Moss, [Garter, Moss, Cable, Moss, Garter], Moss, Cable, Moss, Garter, Moss.

Note: Sleeve sequence will have only one center cable and sequence will finish like this: Moss, Garter, [Moss, Cable, Moss], Garter, Moss.

Use different markers if necessary to help establish patterns and raglan shaping.

Continue increases and patterns until piece from collar measures 9 in / 23 cm (measure length from collar, not length of raglan angle). You should have approx. 114 sts (counting both knit sts for raglan divides) on each front and back, and approx. 82 sts for each sleeve. (It's okay to be off a few sts, don't worry.)

Divide front, back, and sleeves:

Note: Keep track of row you finished so you can start sleeve on proper row.

Work in pattern across front, including knit sts at raglans, place all sleeve sts on a waste yarn. Cast on 12 (16, 20) sts, bypass sleeve, and join to back. Work across back, slip sleeve sts to waste yarn and cast on

12 (16, 20) sts. Place marker, bypass sleeve, and join to front. [276 (292, 308 sts)]

Continue in rounds on front and back [work double moss on 12 (16, 20) added sts] until piece from collar measures 16 (17, 18) in / 40.5 (43, 45.5) cm (or 1½ in / 4 cm less than desired length).

Bottom Ribbing (Multiple of 4)

Change to size US 4 / 3.5 mm circular needle and work in [k2b, p2b] twisted rib for 1½ in / 4 cm (or desired length). Bind off loosely in [k2, p2] rib.

SLEEVES

With 16 in / 40 cm circular, place all sleeve sts from waste yarn on needle. Join yarn and pick up and knit 5 (7, 9) sts from cast-on sts, place marker (this will serve as the beg-of-round marker), pick up 2 sts, place another marker (these 2 sts will always be knit for center underarm), pick up and knit remaining 5 (7, 9) sts, and continue around in pattern. [94 (98, 102) sts]

To work a decrease rnd: Slip marker, k2, slip marker, work2tog (keeping Double Moss pattern correct), work to within 2 sts of end-of-round marker, work 2tog.

Work a decrease rnd every 5th round 17 (17, 19) times to 60 (64, 64) sts.

Sleeve from underarm should measure approx. 12½ (12½, 13½) in / 32 (32, 34.5) cm.

Cuff Ribbing

Change to size US 4 / 3.5 mm needles and work in [k2b, p2b] twisted rib for 1½ in / 4 cm (or desired length). Bind off loosely in [k2, p2] rib.

Make other sleeve to match.

FINISHING

Weave in any loose ends and steam lightly, or block according to directions on ball band.

Woven Stitch Summer Top

Wear this trendy laced-up, strapless cotton top with your favorite jeans or skirt.

SIZES

Juniors 3 (5, 7, 9) (11, 13, 15)
Instructions are written for size 3; all other sizes are in parentheses.

FINISHED MEASUREMENTS

Chest: 29 (32, 34, 35) (35½, 36, 38) in / 73.5 (81.5, 86.5, 89) (90, 91.5, 96.5) cm
Waist: 24 (25½ 26, 27) (28½, 30, 32) in / 61 (65, 66, 68.5) (72.5, 76, 81.5) cm

YARN

Cascade Ultra Pima Fine; 1.75 oz / 50 g each approx. 136.7 yd / 125 m; 100% pima cotton
- 5 (5, 6, 7) (7, 8, 9) skeins #3748 Buttercup (A)
- 1 skein #3728 White (B)

MATERIALS

- Size US 6 / 4 mm 24 in / 60 cm circular needle (*or size to obtain gauge*)
- Tapestry needle
- ¼ in / .6 cm large eyelet kit (grommets)
- 8 ring-type markers
- For I-cord, your choice of purchased lacing material, I-cord machine, or two size US 6 / 4 mm double-pointed needles for hand knitting I-cord

GAUGE

32 sts and 52 rows to 4 in / 10 cm in Woven st

STITCH GUIDE

Wyib. Work with yarn held in back.
Wyif. Work with yarn held in front.

Provisional cast-on. With waste yarn and crochet hook, chain desired number of stitches plus a few more and finish off. Pick up and knit stitches through the back loop of the chain. For those who don't want to crochet, cast on desired number of stitches and knit a few rows in waste yarn before continuing in project yarn.

Special decrease (over 2 rows). RS row: *Work to within 2 sts of marker, knit (or slip) 2 together according to pattern, slip marker, slip (or knit) 2 together. Repeat from *, complete row. *On the next WS row:* Work as established *except* p2tog the 2 slipped sts where they occurred next to the marker on RS.

PATTERN NOTES

- Slipped sts are labeled wyib or wyif (with yarn in back or with yarn in front) and the stitch that follows will be knit or purled in the usual way.
- Peplum and collar are worked separately and stitched to bodice.

BODICE

Begin at bust with 24 in / 60 cm needle and A, cast on 233 (257, 273, 281) (283, 289, 305) sts.

Row 1 (WS): K1, p1, [slip 1 wyib, p1] repeat to last st, k1.

Row 2 (RS): [K1, slip 1 wyif] repeat to last st, k1.

Repeat rows 1 and 2 for Woven Stitch pattern, inserting markers for sides as follows for your size: Work across 58 (64, 68, 70) (71, 72, 76) sts, place marker for side edge, work 117 (129, 137, 141) (141, 145, 153) sts for back, place marker for other side, and finish across row.

Work a special decrease before and after each side marker (4 sts decreased per row) every 12th (10th, 8th, 8th) (10th, 12th, 12th) row 10 (13, 16, 16) (14, 12, 12) times total to 193 (205, 209, 217) (227, 241, 257) sts. *After a decrease row, don't forget to p2tog the slipped sts at each marker from the previous row.*

Work even with no further decreases until bodice measures 9 (9½, 9½, 10) (10½, 11, 11½) in / 23 (24, 24, 25.5) (26.5, 28, 29) cm from beg (or desired length to waist). End having completed a WS row.

Bind off as follows:
(RS): K1, [slip 1, bind off 1, k1, bind off 1] repeat across.

PEPLUM

With A, cast on 392 (404, 434, 441) (453, 465, 507) sts.
Begin Woven st pattern:
Row 1 (WS): K1, p1, [slip 1 wyib, p1] repeat to last st, k1.
Row 2 (RS): [K1, slip 1wyif] repeat to last st, k1.
Row 3: Same as row 1. Place markers for your size as follows: Work 46 (48, 49, 49) (52, 54, 58) sts, place marker, [work 43 (44, 48, 49) (50, 51, 56) sts, place marker] 7 times, work last 45 (48, 49, 49) (51, 54, 57) sts.
Row 4 (RS, special decrease): *Work to within 2 sts of marker, knit (or slip) 2 together according to pattern, slip marker, slip (or knit) 2 together. Repeat from *, complete row. *On the next WS row, work as established except p2tog the 2 slipped sts where they occurred next to the marker on RS. [16 sts decreased].
Work a special decrease row every 4th row 11 (11, 13, 13) (13, 13, 14) times more. *After a decrease row, don't forget to p2tog the slipped sts at each marker from the*

previous row to 200 (212, 210, 217) (229, 241, 267) sts. End having completed a WS row.
Bind off as follows:
(RS): K1, [slip 1, bind off 1, k1, bind off 1] repeat across.

From right side, whipstitch peplum to waist.

Make holes for grommets/large eyelets (overlap fronts, and measure desired distance for desired number of grommets. Poke hole through both layers of fabric with large knitting needle (I used a size 10) and rotate until hole forms through the woven stitch. Push grommet though fabric on RS at the site of the hole and hammer into place. Repeat for each grommet.

COLLAR

With A, cast on 19 sts.
Begin with a WS row and work Woven st until piece measures from just beyond first grommet at front edge, around the back to just before other front grommet.
Whipstitch collar around front from the RS.

FRONT FACING

With A, cast on 27 sts.
Begin with a WS row and work Woven st until piece
measures ¼ in / .5 cm less than distance from bust
to waist at peplum.

I-CORD LACING

With B and double-pointed needles, cast on 4 sts. *Do
not turn work, but bring yarn around the back, slide
work to other end of needle and knit across on RS.
Repeat from * until cord is desired length. To finish,
weave tail through all sts and cinch up before weaving in end on the inside of cord.

FINISHING

Stitch front facing to inside of each front under grommet holes, ¼ in / .5 cm down from top, end at
peplum.
Lace I-cord through grommets, either bottom up or top
down.
Weave in any ends and steam lightly, or block according to directions on ball band.

Zip-Up Hoodie

This traditional-style hooded sweatshirt with cabled detailing on pockets and front is sure to become a go-to piece for just about any occasion. Grommets and I-cord ties add authenticity to this comfortable zip-up sweater.

SIZES

Small (Medium, Large)
Sized to fit Juniors 0–3 (5–9) (11–15)
Instructions are written for size Small; all other sizes are in parentheses.

FINISHED MEASUREMENTS

Chest: 38 (40, 42) in / 96.5 (101.5, 106.5) cm
Length: 22 (22, 24) in / 56 (56, 61) cm

YARN

Cascade 220 Superwash; 3.5 oz / 100 g each approx.
220 yd / 200 m; 100% superwash wool

- 6 (7, 7) skeins #1926 Doeskin Heather (A)
- 1 skein (or approx. 50 yd) #871 White (B, for I-cord tie)

MATERIALS

- Size US 7 / 4.5 mm 24 in / 60 cm circular (*or size to obtain gauge*)
- Size US 4 / 3.5 mm double-pointed needles (for I-cord)
- Tapestry needle
- Waste yarn
- Pin-type markers
- 1 ring-type marker
- 20 (20, 22) in / 51 (51, 56) cm metal separating heavy jacket zipper (available wherever fabric is sold) *Note:* The zipper needs to be 2 in / 5 cm shorter than desired finished length.
- Large eyelet kit (¼ in / .6 cm)
- ½ in / 1.25 cm wide hem tape in color of yarn to cover inside of zipper (optional)

GAUGE

20 sts and 26 rows to 4 in / 10 cm in St st on size US 7 / 4.5 mm needles

STITCH GUIDE

C4B. Place 2 sts on CN and hold at back, k2, then k2 from CN.

C4F. Place 2 sts on CN and hold at front, k2, then k2 from CN.

M1L. From the front, lift horizontal bar between stitch just worked and next stitch, place on needle and knit into the back of it.

M1R. From the back, lift horizontal bar between stitch just worked and next stitch, place on needle and knit into the front of it.

M1P. From the back, lift horizontal bar between stitch just worked and next stitch from the back, place on needle and purl into the front of it.

Three-needle bind-off. Turn pieces inside out and place live stitches on 2 parallel needles. Then knit 2 stitches together, one from each of the parallel needles. Knit another 2 stitches together, one from each needle. You now have 2 stitches on your right needle; use your left needle to pull the first stitch over the second and off the needle (one stitch bound off). Continue binding off in this manner (k2tog, bind off 1).

W&t. Wrap and turn; slip the next stitch, bring the yarn to the front (or back if a purl row), then put the stitch back on the left needle, turn and work back across next row. Some stitches will be left unworked. On the next row, to pick up a wrap on a knit stitch, place needle under wrap first and knit it together with st on needle. To pick up a wrap on a purl stitch, place needle under wrap from behind and put it on left needle, then purl it together with st on needle.

PATTERN NOTES

- Fronts and back worked separately.
- Sleeves picked up and worked flat to cuff.
- Instructions for I-cord and zipper installation included.
- Inch measurements are crucial, as they take into consideration the length of the zipper.

RIGHT FRONT

Note: Set-up row is worked in the usual [k1, p1] rib, then all knit sts of rib are worked through the back loop, all purl sts worked in the usual way. The 12 knit and purl border sts that make up the facing and cable pattern are always worked in the usual way.

Cast on 47 (51, 55) sts.

Set-up row (WS): [P1, k1] repeat to last 12 sts, place marker, [k1, p4, k1, p1, k5].

Row 1 (RS): [P5, k1, p1, k4, p1], slip marker, [k1b, p1] repeat to last stitch, k1.

Row 2 (WS): P1, [k1b, p1] repeat to marker, [k1, p4, k1, p1, k5].

Row 3: [P5, k1, p1, C4B, p1], [k1b, p1] repeat to last stitch, k1.

Row 4: Same as row 2.

Work rows 1–4 until piece from beginning measures 2½ (2½, 3) in / 6.5 (6.5, 7.5) cm. End having completed a WS row.

Next row (begin on row 1 or 3 to keep pattern correct):

Row 1 (RS): [P5, k1, p1, k4, p1], knit to end.

Row 2 (WS): Purl to marker, [k1, p4, k1, p1, k5].

Row 3: [P5, k1, p1, C4B, p1], knit to end.

Row 4: Same as row 2.

To work an increase row on the RS: Work across row as established to last 2 sts, M1L, k2.

To work an increase row on the WS: P2, M1P, work across row as established.

Repeat rows 1–4 and *at the same time* work an increase row every 10th (10th, 11th) row 8 times total to 55 (59, 63) sts.

Work even, if necessary, until piece from beg measures 15 (15, 17) in / 38 (38, 43) cm. End having completed a RS row.

Armhole Shaping

Next row (WS): Bind off 5 sts and work across row. (Hang a pin-type marker somewhere in the middle of the row for ease in measuring.)

Next row (RS): Work in pattern as established to last 3 sts, k2tog, k1.

Next row: Work across.

Work last 2 rows 4 times more to 45 (49, 53) sts. Continue with no further decreases until front from beginning measures 20 (20, 22) in / 51 (51, 56) cm (or length of zipper). End having completed a WS row.

Right Front Neck and Right Shoulder Shaping

Next row (RS): Work across first 12 sts and place on holder or waste yarn and continue across row. (Make note of this row; you'll need this info to work hood later.)

Next 2 rows (WS and RS) Rows 1 and 2: Purl to last 2 sts, w&t, knit back on RS.

Rows 3 and 4: Purl to last 4 sts, w&t, knit back on RS.

Rows 5 and 6: Purl to last 6 sts, w&t, knit back on RS.

Rows 7 and 8: Purl to last 8 sts, w&t, knit back on RS.

Rows 9 and 10: Purl to last 10 sts, w&t, knit back on RS.

Rows 11 and 12: Purl to last 12 sts, w&t, knit to last 4 sts, w&t, purl 12 (15, 18), w&t.

Next 2 rows (RS and WS): Knit across to last 8 sts, w&t, purl 8 (11, 14) (you'll have one stitch wrapped twice), w&t.

Next 2 rows (RS and WS): Knit across to last 12 sts, w&t, work back on WS, picking up wraps and including front 12 from holder.

Work across all sts, picking up remaining wraps as you go. Place 16 (19, 22) sts on a separate holder for shoulder and 29 (30, 31) sts on a holder or waste yarn for hood.

LEFT FRONT

Cast on 47 (51, 55) sts.

Set-up row (WS): [K5, p1, k1, p4, k1], place marker, [p1, k1] repeat to end.

Row 1 (RS): K1, [p1, k1b] repeat to last 12 sts, slip marker, [p1, k4, p1, k1, p5].

Row 2 (WS): [K5, p1, k1, p4, k1] repeat to marker, p1, [k1b, p1] repeat to last st, k1.

Row 3: K1, [p1, k1b] repeat to marker, [p1, C4F, p1, k1, p5].

Row 4: Same as row 2.

Work rows 1–4 until piece from beginning measures 2½ (2½, 3) in / 6.5 (6.5, 7.5) cm. End having completed a WS row.

Begin on a row 1 or 3 to keep pattern correct:

Row 1 (RS): Knit to last 12 sts, [p1, k4, p1, k1, p5].

Row 2 (WS): [K5, p1, k1, p4, k1], purl to end.

Row 3: Knit to last 12 sts, [p1, C4F, p1, k1, p5].

Row 4: Same as row 2.

To work an increase row on the RS: K2, M1L, work across as established.

To work an increase row on the WS: Work across to last 2 sts, M1P, p2.

Repeat rows 1–4 and *at the same time*, work an increase row every 10th (10th, 11th) row 8 times total to 55 (59, 63) sts.

Work even, if necessary, until piece from beg measures 15 (15, 17) in / 38 (38, 43) cm. End having completed a WS row.

Armhole Shaping

Next row (RS): Bind off 5 sts. (Hang a pin-type marker somewhere in the middle of the row for ease in measuring.)

Next row (WS): Work pattern as established to last 3 sts, p2togtbl (through back loop), p1.

Next row (RS): Work across row.

Work last 2 rows 4 times more to 45 (49, 53) sts.

Continue with no further decreases until front from beginning measures 20 (20, 22) in / 51 (51, 56) cm (or length of zipper). End having completed a RS row.

Left Front Neck and Left Shoulder Shaping

Next row (WS): Work across first 12 sts and place on holder or waste yarn and continue across row.

Next 2 rows (RS and WS) Rows 1 and 2: Knit to last 2 sts, w&t, purl back on WS.

Rows 3 and 4: Knit to last 4 sts, w&t, purl back on WS.

Rows 5 and 6: Knit to last 6 sts, w&t, purl back on WS.

Rows 7 and 8: Knit to last 8 sts, w&t, purl back on WS.

Rows 9 and 10: Knit to last 10 sts, w&t, purl back on WS.

Rows 11 and 12: Knit to last 12 sts, w&t, purl to last 4 sts, w&t, knit 12 (15, 18), w&t.

Next 2 rows (WS and RS): Purl to last 8 sts, w&t, knit 8 (11, 14) (you'll have one stitch wrapped twice), w&t.

Next 2 rows (RS and WS): Purl to last 12 sts, w&t, work back on RS picking up wraps and including 12 sts at front from holder.

Purl across all sts, picking up remaining wraps as you go. Work one more row if necessary so both front cables end on the same row. Place 16 (19, 22) sts on a separate holder for shoulders and 29 (30, 31) sts of front on holder or waste yarn for hood.

BACK

Cast on 79 (85, 91) sts.

Set-up row (WS): P1, [k1, p1] repeat across.

Row 1 (RS): K1, [p1, k1b] repeat to last 2 sts, p1, k1.

Row 2 (WS): P1, [k1b, p1] repeat across.

Work rows 1 and 2 until piece from beginning measures 2½ (2½, 3) in / 6.5 (6.5, 7.5) cm. End having completed a WS row.

To work an increase row on the RS: K2, M1L, knit across to last 2 sts, M1L, k2.

To work an increase row on the WS: P2, M1P, purl across to last 2 sts, M1P, p2.

Next row (RS): Working in St st, work an increase row every 10th (10th, 11th) row 8 times total to 95 (101, 107) sts.

Work even, if necessary, until piece from beg measures 15 (15, 17) in / 38 (38, 43) cm. End having completed a WS row.

Armhole Shaping

Next 2 rows: Bind off 5 sts at the beginning of the next 2 rows. (Hang a pin-type marker somewhere in the middle of the row for ease in measuring.)

Next row (RS): K1, ssk, knit to last 3 sts, k2tog, k1.

Next row: Purl.

Work last 2 rows 4 times more to 75 (81, 87) sts.

Continue with no further decreases until armhole measures 7 in / 18 cm. End having completed a WS row.

Back Neck and Left Shoulder Shaping

Next row (RS): Knit 59 (62, 65) sts, place last 43 sts *just worked* on a holder or waste yarn for center back, and knit to last 4 sts, w&t, purl back on WS.

Next row (RS): Knit to last 8 sts, w&t, purl back on WS.

Next row (RS): Knit to last 12 sts, w&t, purl back on WS.

Knit across all sts, picking up wraps as you go. Place sts on a holder or waste yarn.

Right Shoulder Shaping
Join yarn at neck edge on WS, purl to last 4 sts, w&t, knit back on RS.

Next row (WS): Purl to last 8 sts, w&t, knit back on RS.

Next row (WS): Purl to last 12 sts, w&t, knit back on RS.

Purl across all sts, picking up wraps as you go.

Use the three-needle bind-off to connect both sets of 16 (19, 22) shoulder sts from the wrong side.

SLEEVES
At armhole edge, join yarn on RS, and pick up and knit 5 bound-off sts, then 36 sts to shoulder seam, 36 sts to other side, and 5 from bind-off. [82 sts, all sizes]

Place a pin-type marker before and after 12 sts on either side of shoulder seam.

Next row (WS): Purl to first marker, slip marker, purl to second marker, remove marker, w&t, **(RS)** knit to other marker, remove marker and w&t.

Next row (WS): Purl to wrapped st, pick up wrap, w&t, **(RS)** knit to last wrapped st, pick up wrap, w&t.

Repeat last row, working one more st after each w&t on every row until 11 sts remain after last wrapped st at end of knit row. Pick up wrap, but do not turn, k2tog, k9.

Next row (WS): Purl to last 11 sts, pick up wrap and purl wrap and st tog with next st, p2togtbl (through back loop), p9.

Next row (RS): K7, ssk, knit to last 9 sts, k2tog, k7.

Next row (WS): P5, p2tog, p to last 7 sts, p2togtbl (through back loop), p5.

Next row (RS): K3, ssk, knit to last 5 sts, k2tog, k3.

Next row (WS): P1, p2tog, p to last 3 sts, p2togtbl (through back loop), p1. [72 sts remain]

Armhole cap shaping complete.

To work a decrease row on the RS: K2, k2tog, knit to last 4 sts, ssk, k2.

To work a decrease row on the WS: P2, p2togtbl (through back loop), purl to last 4 sts, p2tog, p2.

Work a decrease row every 6th (6th, 7th) row 16 (16, 15) times total to 40 (44, 42) sts. Work even, if necessary, until sleeve from underarm measures 15½ (16, 16½) in / 39.5 (40.5, 42) cm (or 2 in / 5 cm less than desired length). On last RS row, work a k2tog for an odd number of sts for cuff.

Cuff
Next row (WS): P1, [k1b, p1] repeat across.

Next row (RS): K1, [p1, k1b] repeat to last 2 sts, p1, k1.

Repeat last 2 rows until cuff measures 2 in / 5 cm (or desired length). Bind off loosely on RS in pattern.

Make other sleeve to match.

HOOD
Note: Entire hood will keep first and last 12 sts in facing and cable pattern as established. The facing will be turned under to accommodate the zipper on the fronts and the string for the hood.

Join yarn at right front and keeping first 12 sts in facing and appropriate row for cable pattern, work 29 (30, 31) sts from front, then pick up and knit 4 sts from back neck shaping, knit across 21 sts from back, place marker, k1, place marker, knit remaining 21 sts from back neck, pick up and knit 4 sts, then work remaining 29 (30, 31) sts. [109 (111, 113) sts total]

Row 1 (WS): Work first and last 12 sts in cable and facing pattern and purl remaining sts.

Row 2 (RS): Work first and last 12 sts in pattern and knit remaining sts.

To work an increase on the RS: Work to within 1 st of center back marker, M1L, k1, slip marker, k1, M1L, work to end.

Work an increase row every 10th row 5 times and *at the same time* when hood measures approx. 2 in / 5 cm at front, end having completed row 3 of cable pattern.

After the hood measures 2 in, you begin the grommet holes while continuing with directions.

Holes for Grommets

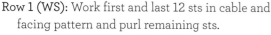

(WS): [K5, p1, k1, p2, yo, p2, k1], purl to last 12 sts, [k1, p2, yo, p2, k1, p1, k5].

Next row (RS): Work as established, dropping yo to make hole for grommet, continue across as established.

Continue working increases every 10th row 4 times.

Work 9 rows.

Next row (RS): Work to within 1 st of center back marker, M1L, remove and replace markers to have 2 sts between them with 58 (59, 60) sts on either side.

Work, if necessary, with no further increases until hood from shoulder seam measures 8 in / 20.5 cm. End having completed a WS row.

Begin Top Shaping

To work decreases on RS: Knit to within 2 sts of first center back marker, ssk, slip marker, k2, slip marker, k2tog, continue around.

Work a decrease row now and every other row 19 (20, 22) times to 80 sts.

Fold hood in half and graft live sts tog to form the top of the hood. (Alternately, you can use the three-needle bind-off from the inside.)

Place grommets over yo holes on the cable and hammer into place. Do not stitch facing yet.

I-CORD

With B and double-pointed needles, cast on 4 sts. *Do not turn work, but bring yarn around the back, slide work to other end of needle, and knit across on RS. Repeat from * until cord is approx. 50 in / 127 cm long or desired length. To finish, weave tail through all sts and cinch up before weaving in end on the inside of cord.

POCKETS

Right Front Pocket

Cast on 20 sts.

To work an increase row on RS: Knit to last st, M1L, k1.

Working in St st and beginning with a purl row, work an increase row every other row 6 times to 26 sts. Purl 1 row.

Next row (RS): Knit to last 3 sts, k2tog, k1.

Next row: Purl.

Repeat last 2 rows 13 times more until 12 sts remain. Work even, if necessary, until total length of pocket is 7 in / 18 cm. Bind off.

Right front pocket cable:
Cast on 12 sts.
Set-up row (WS): K5, p1, k1, p4, k1.
Row 1 (RS): P1, k4, p1, k1, p5.
Row 2: K5, p1, k1, p4, k1.
Row 3: P1, C4B, p1, k1, p5.
Row 4: Same as row 2.
Repeat rows 1–4 until cable fits along outside edge of pocket curve.
Stitch wrong side of facing to the outside edge on RS of pocket, fold over and stitch cable to pocket edge.

Left Front Pocket
Cast on 20 sts.
To work an increase row on RS: K1, M1L, knit to end.
Working in St st and beginning with a purl row, work an increase row every other row 6 times to 26 sts. Purl 1 row.
Next row (RS): Knit 1, ssk, knit to end.
Next row: Purl.
Repeat last 2 rows 13 times more until 12 sts remain. Work even, if necessary, until total length of pocket is 7 in / 18 cm. Bind off.

Left front pocket cable:
Cast on 12 sts.
Set-up row (WS): K1, p4, k1, p1, k5.
Row 1 (RS): P5, k1, p1, k4, p1.
Row 2: K1, p4, k1, p1, k5.
Row 3: P5, k1, p1, C4F, p1.
Row 4: Same as row 2.
Repeat rows 1–4 until cable fits along outside edge of pocket curve.
Stitch wrong side of facing to the outside edge on RS of pocket, fold over and stitch cable to pocket edge.

ZIPPER
Fold facing, from bottom to front neck, to inside and whipstitch into place (leave facing on hood open for later).

Butt zipper teeth next to cable and stitch zipper down on the inside with sewing thread to match color of yarn. Repeat for other side.
If desired, stitch purchased seam binding over back of zipper on inside.

FINISHING
Place pockets on either side of front cable directly over rib and stitch into bottoms, tops, and long sides of pockets into place. Stitch side and underarm seams with a mattress st from the RS.
Thread I-cord through first grommet and wrap around inside perimeter of hood and through second grommet. Stitch facing carefully over cord (do not catch cord), distribute evenly, and tie knots at ends of cord if desired.
Weave in any ends and steam lightly, or block according to directions on ball band.

Abbreviations

Beg	beginning
CN	Cable needle
K	Knit
K1b	Knit into the back loop of the stitch.
K2tog	Knit 2 together.
Kfb	Knit into the front and back of the same stitch
M1	Insert left needle into the horizontal bar that lies between last st worked and next st from the back, then knit into the front of it.
M1L	From the front, lift horizontal bar between stitch just worked and next stitch, place on needle, and knit into the back of it.
M1K	Insert left needle into the horizontal bar that lies between last st worked and next st from the front, then knit into the back of it.
M1P	Insert left needle into the horizontal bar that lies between last st worked and next st from the front, then purl into the back of it.
M1R	From the back, lift horizontal bar between stitch just worked and next stitch, place on needle, and knit into the front of it.
P	Purl
P1b	Purl into the back loop of the stitch.
P2togtbl	Purl 2 together through back loop
Pfb	Purl into the front and back of the same stitch
Psso	Pass the slipped st over
Rnd	Round
RS	Right side
Seed2tog	Keeping the seed stitch pattern correct, knit or purl the next 2 sts together.
Ssk	Slip 2 sts, one at a time knitwise, then insert tip of left needle into the sts on right needle from the front, and complete working two together (left slanting decrease).
St	Stitch
St st	Stockinette stitch
Tog	Together
Tbl	Through back loop
W&t	Wrap and turn; slip the next stitch, bring the yarn to the front (or back if a purl row), then put the stitch back on the left needle, turn and work back across next row. Some stitches will be left unworked.

WS	Wrong side
Yf	Yarn forward; move the yarn in front of the working needle as if to purl.
Yo	Yarn over

CABLE STITCHES

C3B	Slip next st onto CN and hold at back, k2, then k1 from CN.
C3F	Slip next 2 sts onto CN and hold at front, k1, then k2 from CN.
C4B	Slip next 2 sts onto CN and hold at back, k2, then k2 from CN.
C4F	Slip next 2 sts onto CN and hold at front, k2, then k2 from CN.
C5B	Slip next 3 sts onto CN and hold at back, k2, place last st from CN back on left needle and knit it, then k2 from CN.
C6B	Slip next 3 sts onto CN and hold at back, k3, then k3 from CN.
C6F	Slip next 3 sts onto CN and hold at front, k3, then k3 from CN.
C12B	Slip next 6 sts onto CN and hold at back, k6, then k6 from CN.
Cr4L	Slip next 2 sts onto CN and hold at front, p2, then k2 from CN.
Cr4R	Slip next 2 sts onto CN and hold at back, k2, then p2 from CN.
T3B	Slip next 2 sts onto CN and hold at back, p1, then k2 from CN.
T3F	Slip next 2 sts onto CN and hold at front, p1, then k2 from CN.
T4B	Slip next st onto CN and hold at back, k3, then p1 from CN.
T4F	Slip next 3 sts onto CN and hold at front, p1, then k3 from CN.
T5B	Slip next 2 sts onto CN and hold at back, k3, then p2 from CN.
T5F	Slip next 3 sts onto CN and hold at front, p2, then k3 from CN.
T5L	Slip next 3 sts onto CN and hold at front, k2, place last st from CN back on left needle and purl it, then k2 from CN.